How To Speak Furniture With An Antique American Accent

How To Speak Furniture With An Antique American Accent

Buying, Selling and Appraisal Tips Plus Price Guides

Jeanne B. Siegel

Bonus Books, Inc.

749.1
Sie

95 94 93 92 91   5 4 3 2 1

Library of Congress Catalog Card Number: 91-73646

International Standard Book Number: 0-929387-36-8

Bonus Books, Inc.
160 East Illinois Street
Chicago, Illinois 60611

Printed in the United States of America

PURPOSE

The purpose of this book is to provide a comprehensive American furniture language for description, identification, and as a valuable tool in the art of buying, selling, and collecting. The buyer should have the words to ask pertinent questions and the vocabulary to command respect and to use auction catalogs and price guides to their best advantage.

The seller must be able to give customers accurate and beautiful descriptions which many dealers simply don't have at their fingertips.

The "right word" is all important.

Collectors require the ability to describe their collections with loving accuracy.

This book aids in reading other books by taking the mystery out of the words most authors use, but don't explain.

Descriptive words enrich our furniture experience.

This book is dedicated to you, whose heart quickens
at these words

American
Consummate Grace
Beautifully Executed
Nicely Molded
High Styled
Luxuriantly Carved
Rare
Exquisitely Shaped
Well Proportioned
Perfect Balance
Finely Reeded
Bold
Important
Vigorous
Artistic Achievement
Outstanding
Dramatically Executed
Fluent Lines
Family Provenance
Exuberant Expressions
Superlative

and my husband, Jack

CONTENTS

WHY THIS BOOK?

I wrote this book for myself, because this is the book I needed and couldn't find. I searched for one comprehensive guide but did not locate what I sought. I read beautifully photographed and carefully researched texts. They did not provide a complete picture. What is a club foot? Is a snake foot a club foot? Is a claw foot, a claw and ball foot? What is anthemia? How can I quickly differentiate an American Hepplewhite chair from an English one? How is a Hepplewhite sideboard distinguished from a Sheraton sideboard? Is it birch or mahogany? What is that "do-hickey" on the crest-rail called? What is a "turkey-breast" cupboard? A "let-in" table top? A "rain gutter"? "Breadboard ends"? Wonderful descriptive terms like these cannot be found in the dictionary.

I carefully studied surveys that had limited information and books that were extremely complicated, covering history, revivals, and "museum pieces" that most of us encounter only in museums; some that separated tables, chairs, and casepieces in separate volumes. Many gave only American dates and not parallel English & French ones, and not always the name of the period. Museums seldom give periods on their descriptions either. Many give name, country of origin, date, wood and no other information. Example: desk, American, circa 1710. It would be considerably enlightening if style, characteristics, wood and brasses were noted. Example: Desk, American, block and shell carved center drawer flanked by columned document drawers, scrolled bracket feet, striped tiger maple, willow brasses not original.

I am convinced that proper furniture description is absolutely imperative. Unfortunately this is a skill many dealers lack. This important ability can enable an intelligent person to effectively judge a dealer, use price guides and auction sheets to his best advantage, understand ads, and to see with an educated eye.

First I wrote a simple introduction to American furniture. Next I put together one and two liners pointing out characteristics, clues, and "bewares". These are short but hopefully they will be interesting, perhaps fun, and might save a person grief. I believe anyone can deal with the eight major periods of American furniture if

1

they understand or have access to this American furniture vocabulary.

Each period can be referred to separately. The major pieces, key words, decorations, characteristics, woods, brasses and important cabinetmakers are covered. Illustrations are in each section. If we readily know the major periods in their proper order we can place transitional pieces.

My vocabulary is a "labor of love". It is the heart of this book. I define words dealing with and describing American furniture. Their European counterparts are also included. The study of American furniture requires a vocabulary, similar to the study of a new language such as Spanish or computer. English and French words are used to describe American furniture. Should an American table be called a "demi-lune"? With each word I give the meaning, examples where it appears, and in what periods.

In the glossary I point out details. A geometric half round stylized shell with carved rays, found primarily on Queen Anne pieces, is called a "fan", a "rising sun" or a "sunrise". In England the same carving is called a "sunburst". Benjamin Franklin in a discussion with James Madison, said it was definitely a sunrise! When pressed he assured Madison that he had observed many of these decorations and could state without doubt that it was a sunrise and not a sunset. I for one would not consider contradicting him. I find it interesting that a certain American Federal style open armchair is called a "Martha Washington" chair, while the English counterpart is referred to as a "Gainsborough" chair, after the great English portrait painter who posed many of his subjects in them. Do you find it interesting that underturned Spanish feet from our William and Mary period were inspired by bound feet seen on Oriental women? I hope that if such information interests me, it will perhaps interest you.

I include auction terms, dealers' words, slang, repair terms, double meanings, alternate terms, timber information, and decoration words like "chinoiserie" and "shaker red".

Finally I hope this book helps in reading other books and takes the mystery out of the words some authors take for granted.

My deepest appreciation is reserved for Jeanne Federico, former Director of the D.A.R. Museum in Washington D.C. After hearing Carol Vannover, a docent at the Chicago Art Institute, praise the D.A.R. and their wonderful director, I took a chance. I called Jeanne and described what I was working on and that I needed additional research. Jeanne simply said, "when do you want to come?" Her expertise and total familiarity with every piece in the museum is a joy. I urge everyone to visit this superb museum. It is a love song to America built by the female descendents of Revolutionary War officers. This gem collection has thirty period rooms and an important decorative arts collection. It is properly located at 1776 D. Street.

My thanks to the Smithsonian Museum, with a special thanks to Ann Serio who kindly allowed me access to the storerooms, card files, and picture gallery. This is a great National Treasure. Winterthur in Wilmington, Delaware was another journey filled with learning and pleasure. Also, the DeWitt Wallace Museum in Virginia, the American Wing of the Metropolitan in New York, the Baltimore Museum of Art, the Maryland Historical Society, and the Walters Museum in Baltimore provided additional learning experiences. The American Museum in Bath, England is one of the finest museums of American furniture in the world. More thanks to the Milwaukee Art Museum, the Chicago Historical Society and the Chicago Art Institute. I am grateful to Antiques Magazine and to Wendell Garrett for graciously allowing me the use of certain photographs. Others from Sotheby Parke Bernet in New York and from Michael Corbett of the Federalist in Kenilworth, Illinois were very valuable. Many thanks to Georgia Burnett who paid me to learn and enjoy myself.

Finally, my thanks to Claudette Fortman whose excellent typing made the manuscript readable.

INTRODUCTION TO
ANTIQUE AMERICAN FURNITURE

American furniture masterpieces were made by gifted carpenters in their own workshops. They were made for the "best people". The best people were not kings, queens, princes, or lords. These wonderful functional pieces were for actual use in the homes of important colonial Americans.

Americans did not have a monopoly on simple furniture, but they made their finest furniture simple. This simplicity was uniquely American! The finest furniture of other countries is ornate. In comparison American furniture stands out with quiet elegance and vital individuality. American craftsmanship, exhibited in Rhode Island Chippendale block and shell pieces, is a symbol of American pride and accomplishment.

In Europe, furniture made in the smaller towns copied but simplified the "court pieces" of London and Paris. These pieces are called "country furniture". Americans made the finest "country pieces" of all.

Anyone truly fascinated with antique American furniture should study the history of furniture in general and English and French furniture in particular. It is a spellbinding journey to follow the recycling of designs throughout history. Assurbanipal, an Assyrian king, lounged on couches with lathe-turned legs not unlike couches early Americans rested on in the William and Mary period. Tutankhamen's paw-footed throne survives on Sheraton pieces made by the great Duncan Phyfe. Tut's throne was painted and so were American Pennsylvania Dutch pieces and American Empire Hitchcock chairs. Early Puritan turned chairs can be mistaken for earlier Scandinavian turned chairs. Brasses from the Orient are the origin of brass handles used on colonial casepieces. On and on...English furniture reflected these many influences and as a result American furniture is a microcosm of furniture history.

London was the "mecca" we looked to for furniture guidance. This was due to the language and culture bond and because we truly admired English taste. With American "know-how" we adapted English styles to our needs and resources. For example, Benjamin Franklin put rockers on a Windsor chair and created a uniquely

American piece. The world had centuries of cradles but it took an American to design the rocking chair.

Three of our major furniture periods are named for English designers. They are Thomas Chippendale, George Hepplewhite, and Thomas Sheraton. Amazingly, none of these genuises were considered "crown worthy". Hepplewhite had the Prince of Wales as a customer, but not Mama.

In studying and comparing American antique furniture with English or French of the same period, the same period is later in America. It took time for a style to travel from London to Paris to the towns and then to cross the ocean. The wealthier the Englishman or Frenchman, the fancier and more ornate his furniture. These extremely decorated pieces can be identified without difficulty. However, many beautiful pieces must be carefully studied to determine their true origin.

America created no original major furniture period of her own. There were of course, many original American pieces, the most important coming from Newport, Rhode Island in the Chippendale period. Shaker furniture had its own singular character but was of English origins and was not a major period.

New Americans brought few pieces of furniture to the new world. Therefore, the colonists put in "rush orders" for household needs. American craftsmen did not have unlimited time to produce furniture as their English counterparts had. The English guilds, known for their exclusivity were also known for their slowness. Our furniture makers were joiners, carpenters, apprentices and indentured servants. Ship's carpenters when in port often turned their hands to furniture making. The guild system had not crossed the Atlantic. So our wonderful furniture heritage stems from the bold individual creativity of the American craftsman versus the English guild "production line" approach. Proof of that creativity is found in the masterpieces of men like Thomas Affeck of Philadelphia, Benjamin Randolph of Philadelphia, Benjamin Frothingham of Massachusetts, William Savery of Philadelphia, Thomas Needham of Massachusetts, Duncan Phyfe of New York, John, Job and Daniel Townsend of Newport, Rhode Island, and John Goddard, also from Newport. The colonists wanted their furniture fashionable, but in keeping with the size of their homes and their lifestyles. Fashion was very important to these early Americans.

As styles of English furniture changed, American furniture also changed. For example, English and subsequently American furniture in the period 1690 to 1720 was influenced by Dutch styles. Hence the William and Mary period. Trade with the Orient resulted in brass pulls, lacquering, caning, and cabriole legs on both English, and American furniture. Although American furniture styles came from England with Dutch, Flemish, and Chinese influences (and after the Civil War from French styles), you will find a variety of styles in addition to the dominant ones. Examples are Pennsylvania German painted pieces from Pennsylvania and Ohio, and Spanish colonial furniture from New Mexico.

But whatever influenced American furniture, it always retained its tendency towards simplicity. In the English William and Mary period, inverted cup-turning on table legs were often pierced with open carving similar to the Oriental ivories the English admired. American inverted cup-turnings were solid and plain. In the Empire period the Americans often substituted simple stencil gilding for ornate ormolu.

Practically every book dealing with American furniture states "We are a young country and can reach back and touch our roots". When I read this I would think about the Continental Congress sitting on painted Windsor chairs or historical movies showing the pilgrims and Indians grouped around a trestle table. But when a stunning Oriental woman came into the antique store where I worked, this "young country bit" really sank in. She succinctly stated she was Chinese, had lived in Taiwan, could speak English beautifully, and had come to buy her husband an antique American desk. After she looked at three fine pieces and favored one in particular, I began to tell her about its history. But as soon as I mentioned its age, about one hundred and seventy years, she backed away towards the door. When she reached it, she turned and looked at me reproachfully and said, "I told you I wanted an antique desk and this one isn't even old".

The human need for change is very apparent in the study of furniture. High-carved furniture will likely regain favor simply because it has been out of fashion for five generations. With neo-classical features in architecture again assuming great importance it is reasonable to assume neo-classical furniture will also regain popularity. The eight major periods however do not change. Our perception of what is "in" does. A few years ago even Duncan Phyfe pieces had to wait for a "good home". Whether we collect, inherit, sell or just admire antique American furniture, it is a pleasure to look at and a pleasure to learn about. It is a way to understand American values and perhaps ourselves.

CHICANERY AND CLUES

Anything an old cabinetmaker could do, craftsmen can still do! I repeat, anything an old craftsman could do can still be done!

The more you handle antiques, touch, measure with your eyes, rub your fingers across and mentally photograph, the quicker you'll develop instinct. Instinct is very real. I know unless I see "a dry martini" in the dome of an antique French paperweight or "cold velvet" in old marble I back off. Whatever visual trick works for you, use it. When your bell rings, listen!

Love seats can be made from the four legs of an antique chair. The new parts are hidden under the upholstery. If an exposed seat rail is part of the design, old bed-boards can be used. Elementary, my dear Watson.

Antique stool legs, that have shorter legs than ordinary chair legs, can be employed to construct expensive wing chairs that had short legs. This is why it is preferable to buy an antique frame and have it upholstered.

Pie-crusts can be added to plain topped tables. Always feel the edges. If they feel sharp, look closely. Look closely at all sharp edges! Antique furniture edges look "lived-in".

Table legs were often changed to conform to current tastes. Fine antique pieces had their perfect original legs changed if certain dealers thought they could sell for more money. Crawl underneath and feel for filled in holes. Suggest less money if you still want the piece. Carry a flashlight.

Misrepresenting the origin of a piece for profit is a form of fakery. For example, when a knowledgeable dealer sells an English side chair as a more valuable Massachusetts side chair.

Beautiful William and Mary and Queen Anne highboys have been turned into chests with bracket feet to provide "early chests". If all the parts are genuine it's almost impossible to spot.

Flat top tall pieces have been converted to more valuable scroll-top pieces. A clue is evident in the heavy horizontal board dovetailed into the vertical dividers above the center top drawer. Check the back for splotches of stain behind the questionable area.

8

Early chamber or commode chairs have been transformed by removing the deep skirt and replacing the knee brackets. I can't totally fault this practice.

Always buy from a shop's owner if possible. An assistant usually cannot lower the price very much. Often the owner will, depending on the original cost to him, how long it has been unsold or if a loan was required to buy it. It doesn't hurt to bargain.

Old furniture shrinks because wood is 80% to 90% water. Round tables are no longer symmetrically round. Drawers may no longer fit perfectly. Inlay shows shrinkage. This is proper.

Oval drop-leaf tables with the leaves too close to the floor may be altered rectangular drop-leaf tables. Oval drop-leaf tables being more readily saleable, oval pieces were substituted to replace existing rectangular leaves. A leaf with two timbers is questionable as leaves were usually a single piece. If a table reminds you of a basset hound, check the leaves.

Holes that serve no purpose indicate a substitute piece. A small knitting needle serves me well.

Carry a tape measure!

One authentic antique member with all other parts new does not make an antique. The one fine part is of course remarked on. "The patina on the seat is so mellow."

One antique piece can be "twined" to make two antique pieces. Check both sides of a piece.

Popular pieces like pine cupboards make me wonder how so many survived. Put me in the "doubtful column". You can be sure that many are new fakes or new fakes made with some old wood members. A little gesso rubbed on the knots does not make a piece old. I've seen "antiques" with fresh sawdust still clinging.

Sunlight bleaches wood within weeks. Leave a glass paperweight on a piece in direct sunlight and you'll see.

A pile of manure (ammonia) placed near furniture ages it rapidly.

Living insects eat wood exactly like their ancestors (worm holes). Living forgers also use icepicks and various sized nails.

Old keys and wire brushes and tools called chippers age furniture fast. Chippers look like small cleavers and are worked over furniture surfaces to simulate age. They do! So do dirty snow chains.

Signs of wear should be in proper places! This is important!

Splotches of stain are a warning. Check the area very carefully! Inside and out. Has the area been repaired, remodeled or replaced?

Layers of bees-wax contribute to the look and aroma of antique. Don't allow "antique perfume" to sway your senses.

A blowtorch ages wood by darkening it irregularly and the piece looks truly aged.

Dirty furniture looks older than clean furniture.

Various fire-screen tripods have been recycled as tea or tilt and turn tables. If the proportions of a tripod piece appear "off" stay away from it or suggest a lower price.

When I hear "there's a piece just like it in the XYZ Museum" I wonder. If a dealer has such a rare piece, why am I being offered it? Wouldn't an auction with many potential buyers offer greater rewards? Reproductions are very like museum pieces, while authentic pieces seldom are.

Look at furniture you are considering purchasing in good light. If possible take the piece outside.

Look at all sides of a piece. The legs, inside, bottom, top and back, including the cornice or pediment. Ask for the use of a ladder if necessary.

Remove all drawers. The inside condition will indicate repairs, remodeling and changes!

People who don't look carefully might find "made in Holland" on the backboard after they get it delivered. This really happened to a red-faced dealer.

Ask to have all known repairs pointed out. If a piece has "in the rough" on it, this means it is in need of work.

Three-ply veneer is modern so antique pieces shouldn't have any.

Early screws are one-half inch or even shorter and have flat heads and flat tips and uneven threads.

Old screws are difficult to turn and may be rusted in. Beware of loose screws. Tips remain blunt up to 1850. After 1850 the screw tips were pointed.

Old handmade nails are forged, as in furnace, and so are of different sizes. They are not uniform. They are not all alike. They are called "rose-headed". Old nails often bleed on wood around the nail hole.

Old dowels, wooden pins, are not uniformly round. Those produced by machines are.

Marks from antique ripsaws are straight. Modern saws make half-moon impressions. Tilt pieces upside down and at an angle to see these impressions. The impression left on a timber by a saw is called a kerf mark.

Antique saws can still be used to make furniture, but not antiques.

New paint is not as hard as old paint. It dents.

Old paint looks softer than new paint.

Old paint has a mottled patina.

Old paint can shatter into slivers.

Grain painting is the technique of applying paint to imitate the grain of wood. This was first done in America in the Puritan period. Grain painting has a long English history.

An 18th century chair splat fits into a shoe, (two pieces) above the seat rail. A 19th century chair splat incorporates the splat and shoe. (one piece).

Early dovetails were not carbon copies of each other. Later dovetails have identical and uniform shapes. Dovetails can be seen on ancient Egyptian pieces. We still use them.

Are American dovetails distinctive? No. Even Newport, Rhode Island dovetails which come to a point as they near the face of a drawer are not singular. Similar ones are found on English pieces.

The two basic forms of corner blocks (seat bracing) found on American chairs both appear on English chairs.

On most American chairs, the knee brackets are deep and glued between the bottom of the seat-rail and the knee of the leg. In England it is usual to have the piece of wood forming the seat-rail drop down behind the bracket. This English trait is also found on various Philadelphia chairs.

Antique chests have more than three drawers.

Do not believe what you want to believe. No one can fool us like we can fool ourselves!

Brasses should match the period, even if not original. (In each period I review the brasses of the period.) Brasses should also match the original holes on the piece. Check to see if the original holes have been filled in.

If the original brasses (mounts) survive, and this is rare, carefully removing one will disclose the original finish. This can be very exciting! Mounts were referred to as "brass furniture" by both Colonial American and English merchants. Many have engraved catalog numbers on their reverse side.

If the finish underneath the mount (the brasses) is identical to the outside, it has recently been refinished. If possible, ask to have one brass removed.

The edge of the brass plate will leave a scar in the surface of an old piece.

Early brasses are a light yellow color.

Antique brasses were meant to be kept brightly polished. As rooms were lighted and heated by the fireplace, early Americans enjoyed the firelight reflecting and offering glowing counterpoints of this light on their brasses. Even the rich used candles very sparingly.

English brasses can be much larger and more ornate than those made for the American trade. The exception is the brasses used on Newport, Rhode Island block and shell pieces in the Chippendale period.

While brasses were mainly manufactured in England until

the Hepplewhite period, some colonists like Paul Revere produced their own.

Yes, there are forged labels. Labels are easy to produce or reproduce. Easier than ever with new copying equipment and new grime. Remember to look carefully at the piece and judge on merit.

Old newspapers or memorabilia have been known to find their way into newer pieces. This is called salting.

Provenances can be written with a little knowledge of history, imagination, and a quill pen. On the other hand, checking out a provenance can be exciting, and you might have a very interesting experience. It is amazing, but true, that many families kept the original bills of sale. Always keep your receipts!

For yourself, your heirs, and your insurance company, ask for a written description, history and price, if possible under the dealer's letterhead. This is also helpful if a piece is damaged by a moving company.

Most dealers keep a polaroid camera on hand; if so ask for a picture.

Branded signatures are duplicated by kinky persons with ease and a branding iron.

The Hitchcock stenciled signature is a simple exercise to "stencil", and could raise the price. If the signature is on a fairly priced chair, it's "frosting on the cake". Is the price fair? Check recent price guides.

Check the lines of the chair. Is it really a Hitchcock? I see "Hitchcocks" that aren't. On the other hand people have bought "Hitchcocks" that aren't, but much more valuable Sheraton "fancy chairs". A little luck can't hurt.

Beware of revival pieces made after 1876!!! These 19th century pieces hopefully will not be sold to you as original pieces. You say "they are old now". True, but they are not original and I hope you do not pay original prices for these pieces. These revival pieces were not made as fakes, but as copies. Many are very much like the originals. Others have dowels where no dowels were originally used. Often the dimensions are wrong and the weight is too light. Some of these pieces are real foolers.

Be cautious at private sales (like house sales). They can be salted with phonies by the private party or by the sale agent, especially at an impressive home. Not all auctions are legitimate either. I urge you to read "Auction Madness" by Charles Hamilton.

Appreciate dealers with fine reputations who have remained in business for many years. If an honest mistake is made or if you want to upgrade or sell back, reputable dealers will try to oblige.

If a piece has "your name on it" you'll get it. Some things are meant. Some aren't.

CHARACTERISTICS

Drawers tell a lot about a casepiece. American drawers were constructed with thick boards of poplar, pine and chestnut. Drawer bottoms of poplar may have a distinctive greenish stripe. American Queen Anne and American Chippendale drawer bottoms were often of white cedar that resembles pine with small knots.

English drawers were constructed with thinner boards of oak or deal. Deal is thin boards of scotch fir that is also called wild pine. English drawers almost without exception have thin oak bottoms.

American casepieces, with the exception of various Williamsburg Virginia and Charleston South Carolina pieces, did not have dust boards placed between the drawers. Dustboards are large pieces of wood placed between the drawers to prevent stealing from a locked drawer by putting a hand through an unlocked one.

English casepieces have dustboards.

Were Americans more honest? More trusting? Too busy to bother?

The insides of American casepieces, undersides, and backs were not waxed, varnished, stained or painted.

Exposed backboards darken with age but enclosed drawers do not.

English pieces repaired here will have the thick American woods. So if you are identifying a piece with drawers, check each one. At the same time check for dustboards.

Large American pieces such as secretaries or highboys are seldom as large as English ones.

English casepieces are usually taller and wider than American.

American furniture parts, called members, are usually heavier and sturdier than English parts.

American furniture is generally less adorned and decorated than English or French pieces.

American carving is not as deep or as detailed as that found on English and French pieces.

The latest characteristics on a piece determine its period.

Panel chests with lids of solid timbers are probably American.

English panel chests usually had panelled lids.

Domed top chests are probably Continental.

Panel chests featuring linen-fold carving are probably English. Both Americans and Britons sometimes painted their furniture.

Early cedar gate-leg tables are English.

Heavily carved wainscot chairs are English.

English Jacobean cupboards often used carved griffins or mythical creatures as supports. American Puritan cupboards used only bulbous turnings. Our griffins came in the Empire period.

English Jacobean pieces might have pearl inlays. American Puritan pieces did not.

William and Mary cane chairs with animal feet are English.

William and Mary cane topped tables are English.

Square cabriole legs are not American. They are found on English William and Mary pieces.

Twisted or spiral furniture legs were found in both England and America. However, they were more common in England. American twisted legs say "New York", but some were made in Philadelphia.

William and Mary cane chairs with faces on their knees are English.

Another English trait in the William and Mary period is double-domed tops on tall casepieces like secretaries.

American Queen Anne secretaries usually had solid wood doors in their upper portion. Queen Anne secretaries inset with looking-glass say "English". However, as all furniture was commissioned there are examples of glass in American pieces. But this is very rare.

English Queen Anne chairs sometimes terminate the rear legs

in squared hoof feet. This is not an American trait.

Various English Queen Anne chairs have modified block Spanish feet on the rear legs. Americans used the Spanish foot only on the front legs.

English Queen Anne pad feet are more circular than ours.

Pointed pad feet suggest New Jersey.

Cabriole legs standing on realistic hoof feet with carved fetlocks indicate English origin.

American Queen Anne slipper feet indicate New York and Rhode Island.

Cabochons with foliage are found on English 1740's cabriole legs at the knee. Americans didn't favor cabochons on their knees, but some, usually smaller, appear on certain Philadelphia Chippendale chairs and also on a variety of American and English Victorian pieces.

Early English Windsors are light in weight, have straight "D" shaped seats, and straight plain turned legs. In these early chairs you can see the English base of American Shaker furniture.

If you see a Windsor chair with downturned scrolling crest-rail ears (volutes) it is American. This trait is uniquely American!

English Windsors often had colt (hoof) feet; not an American trait.

Early English Windsors were painted (often green), not stained. The same is true for American Windsors.

English Windsors often had pierced ornamental back splats. American ones usually had backs composed entirely of spindles. Occasionally some are seen with arches.

English Windsors often had cabriole legs with pad feet. American Windsors did not except in very rare instances.

Late English Windsors became much larger, and heavier, and top-heavy, and more complex, than contemporary American ones of the period.

Rocking chairs are uniquely American! Ben Franklin invented them.

Pierced pie-crust tables are English.

Bombe chests are a Boston or Salem Massachusetts design.

Ribbon-back Chippendale style chairs are English. These very fancy chairs were not made in America. A simpler ribbon design was made in Maryland, Pennsylvania and New York.

Americans did not carve monsters on their furniture until the late Victorian period, and then not as heavily or often as the English.

In the Empire period we did carve winged griffins, winged lions, sea horses, swans, dolphins, caryatids, and "mummy headed therms", on our furniture.

New York Chippendale chair splats used strapwork enclosing a diamond.

New York Chippendale chairs are squarer and heavier than most American chairs in this period. Their claw and ball feet are also squarer.

Philadelphia favored the tasselback Chippendale splat.

Philadelphia wing chairs occasionally had carved masks on their aprons.

Queen Ann Pennsylvania high chests from 1760, Newport Chippendale tall pieces and various Connecticut highboys are known to have detachable legs. While this trait is considered American, we also find English tall pieces with this detail. They were easier to move or ship with the legs off.

Beautifully carved roses on French pieces indicate Louis XVI because Marie Antoinette loved them. So did John Belter in the American Victorian period.

English and American tall chests in the Chippendale and Federal periods frequently had friezes and cornices at the top, often employing fret-work. The English pieces were often more elaborate.

Carving on English Chippendale claw and ball feet are usually more richly detailed than American.

Exaggerated knees on cabriole legs with claw and ball feet indicate "revival pieces". Pieces made after 1876. Look carefully if this trait appears.

Claw and ball feet with thin claws, the inside one curving backward, say "Massachusetts".

Mahogany arm chairs in the Chinese manner with triple cluster column legs, perhaps with a pagoda shaped top-rail, are English.

American Chippendale side chairs from states that had slaves did not have carving on their backs, and if upholstered had cheap material on the backs, the rationale being that only slaves saw the chair backs. Side chairs when not in use stood with their backs to the wall.

American Chippendale secretaries generally had paneled wood doors in their upper section. This trait continued from the Queen Anne period.

The English Chippendale style secretaries continued to favor looking glass-doors or glass doors.

Chippendale tripod pie-crust tables with the entire "pie" carved to resemble a Chinese dish are English.

Chippendale tripods have upturned feet while Hepplewhite tripods have tapered toes.

English Hepplewhite commodes had painted decoration and elaborate marquetry and gilt brass (ormolu) mounts. American Hepplewhite pieces were much plainer.

American Hepplewhite chair-shields stand well above the back-rail, but the shield is lower on English Hepplewhite chairs.

Chairs with carved spade feet are English. Both England and America had Hepplewhite spade feet. Ours were always plain.

Certain Hepplewhite chairs have inlaid cuffs on their legs. This trait is American and English.

A Federal table with tapered legs and a scalloped gallery will probably be Hepplewhite.

An open arm, upholstered high-back chair in the American Chippendale and Federal periods is often called a "Martha Washington" chair. Its English sibling is called a "Gainsborough" chair after the famous English portrait painter who sat many of his subjects in this type of chair.

If the ends of the curve are concave on a Federal style sideboard it is a Hepplewhite piece.

If the ends of the curve are convex on a Federal style sideboard it is a Sheraton piece.

On American Sheraton sideboards the handle bases are usually oval. On English Sheraton sideboards the handle bases are usually round.

Many English Sheraton pieces combined gilt, inlay, and complete paintings, often by famous artists of the period like Angelia Kauffman, Cipriana, and Pergolese. Ours never reached this degree of decoration.

English painted chairs parallel to our Sheraton period often had upholstered seats. American painted "fancy chairs" did not have this trait.

Observe furniture heights. If you know an antique American Sheraton "Martha Washington" chair is approximately 47 inches high, a shorter one should raise questions. If it is higher you might consider English origin. (American chair seats are about 16 to 18 inches high. Rocking chair seats about 14 to 16 inches high. Victorian rocking chair seats about 12 inches high.)

Reeded cup-turnings appear at the upper portion of some English Sheraton tapered legs. American Sheraton legs do not have this trait.

Low-back upholstered Sheraton arm-chairs were common in England but not in America.

It is not unusual to find American Empire pieces that are larger than French Empire pieces.

Empire pieces with military ormolu are French.

When in doubt rococo revival furniture is curvy, renaissance revival furniture is angular, Elizabethan revival has barley sugar twists, and gothic revival has pointed arches.

In the American Victorian period, we used grotesque masks, lion heads, hounds, stags, cupids, putti, and occasionally a sphinx head. The corresponding English period used more of everything.

The American Victorian secretary is built in one piece. This characteristic is unique. The piece is French influenced.

America began jappaning furniture in the William and Mary period.

American chinoiserie designs came form Oriental plates or design books.

Americans particularly liked blue-green grounds decorated with red, green, and gold gilt.

The English of the parallel-Georgian period preferred vermillion and dark green grounds. They added varnish to the ground colors for brilliance. Americans did not share this trait but as always there are exceptions to the rule.

American and English jappaned pieces are also seen with black and brown grounds and both used tortiose-shell grounds.

Japanese artists used forty to fifty coats of lacquer. The English used two. American pieces as usual have even less. They were usually thinly jappaned, and some even have designs on bare wood.

English jappaned pieces were heavily decorated while ours are simply done with a light hand. Our most decorated jappaned pieces were made in Boston, Philadelphia, and New York in the Chippendale period.

English pieces have their chinoiserie designs built up with gesso. We did not use gesso, but occasionally used whiting. (crushed chalk).

English jappaned pieces were often displayed on ornately carved and gilded stands and might have carved matching tops. Not an American trait.

WOODS

The identification of woods is not an easy task. Museums often have a question mark on their card files.

American Tories carried American-made furniture back to England when they returned because of the Revolutionary War. Much was New York furniture. New York pieces copied English furniture closely and clearly reflected the dominance of Loyalists in the city's population. Therefore antique American furniture has resided there since that time. (The American Museum in Bath, England has one of the world's finest collection of antique American furniture)

Many fine antique English pieces were made of American Virginia walnut. It was exported to England beginning in 1720. English forests were worked out and the "great fire" of London in 1656 had destroyed existing furniture, buildings, and lumberyards within the city. This catastrophe was a motivating force for companies like the "South Sea Company" to sponsor the colonies to secure a source of lumber.

Considerable English furniture made of Virginia walnut, which dates about 1720 to 1760, is mistaken for mahogany. This is because this wood has little figure and is a dark color. Perhaps it was stained and polished a dark red color to resemble mahogany. One way to tell the difference is that walnut grays from sunlight. Another is that the insides of a mahogany piece will show a pink tone.

Furniture pests still invade furniture. They can eat an arm or leg hollow. The member eventually cracks and a grayish powder spills out (dry rot). An expert must clean out the diseased area and fill it in or replace the part. Some refinishing is also called for. Check cracks carefully.

Wood-burning fireplaces and later coal fires darkened wood tones.

Old timbers can be extremely wide. Old mahogany trees produced twelve foot wide timbers.

Old timbers were not uniform in width.

Timbers are strongest along the grain.

Backboards on antique casepieces were made of random width timbers and are often rough.

Veneer is a thin layer of wood glued to a base wood. In America veneering was first used in the William and Mary period.

Marquetry is actually a sophisticated form of veneering. It was first employed as a furniture detail in our William and Mary period.

Marquetry with ivory, dyed woods or bone are likely to be Continental rather than English or American.

Old hand cut veneers can be nearly 1/8 inch thick. Since 1840, machine cut veneers are 1/32 to 1/64 of an inch thick. The newer veneers hold more securely because glues hold the thinner veneers better. Animal glues were used on antique pieces. Today many synthetic polyvinal resin adhesives are employed.

Burl veneer is the growth from a tree trunk sliced and glued to a wood base.

Crotch-grain means veneer generally cut from the main crotch or fork of a tree.

Old wood develops soft, warm color hues.

A natural patina, which is the furniture surface, is even in color and has a mellow quality.

Poorly restored pieces will appear harsh compared with naturally aged antique pieces.

Splotches of stain say a patina is not natural. Look for repairs, restoration or replacements.

French polishing means shellacked with a glass like finish. It is flashier than a natural patina and might appear cloudy. French polishing was not done when the piece was originally built.

French polishing of walnut can turn the mellow tone to a red henna-like tint and streaks may result.

French polishing also affects the patina of other woods. Birch that has been French polished may also exhibit reddish streaks.

Do not strip an old piece unless there is no other way to restore it! Many furniture refinishers have no soul and less sense! Explore every alternative first. The value and beauty of the piece will suffer greatly if the natural patina is totally removed! Antique furniture should not look "like new"!

Soft woods and maple turn a little honey-brown with age.

Walnut, birch, maple, cherry, and gum were often stained to look like mahogany.

A walnut stain was also used to make mahogany, cherry and maple a rich brown color.

Birch was often stained to resemble maple, cherry, gum, mahogany, and walnut. For this reason it is called the "chameleon of woods". Much Federal period "satinwood" was really birch.

Walnut, mahogany, and satinwood darken with age unless faded from the sun.

Walnut grays from sunlight.

Mahogany does not gray from exposure to sunlight.

Walnut timbers may produce markings of stripes, waves, and mottles.

Red walnut ages to brandy hues.

Victorian black walnut was created by applying a stain or acid to walnut which had any red tinge and was then stained very dark.

Mahogany has plain figures and swirl grains. Timbers show stripe, dark elliptical markings called "plum pudding", fiddle-back, mottle, blister, and dark flakes called "roe".

Mahogany was stained a deep reddish color in the Empire period in America and France.

Pine may turn brown, or even black from years of waxing.

Pine may become grayish-white or bleached from years of scrubbing. We often see this on kitchen tables.

Southern pine can be identified by its alternating clear and pitch wood.

Southern yellow pine has an almost purplish cast.

Southern yellow pine is also called "heart pine" because furniture was made from the center of the timber.

Maple stained cherry is difficult to identify from actual cherry. Cherry is heavier. Cherry pieces are often more expensive.

Cherry browns with age. Its grain is straight.

Cherry is perhaps the most beautiful American wood and the most undervalued.

Figures are timber designs brought out by cutting the wood so veneers or solid surfaces display various types of irregularities in the grain and in color.

Maple figures include fiddle-back, curly or tiger stripes, blister which are "wart-like", and bird's eye markings.

Fiddle-back figures are primarily found in Honduras mahogany.

Black cherry has a mild ring growth figure.

Applewood is hard, closegrained, light to medium pinkish tan, with distinctive knots and streaks or bands of darker pigmentation that looks like spilled black coffee.

Oak resembles chestnut, hickory, and ash. They all have distinct pores. Chestnut, however, does not have the rays that oak does.

American oak can retain its golden color while English oak usually darkens.

Old English oak has a coarse raised grain that you can feel with your fingertips.

The English made entire pieces from satinwood. We did not.

Yew wood is English. Don't confuse it with fruitwoods or red cedar. It is orangish in color.

Holly wood is white and ideal for dyeing. New Jersey holly was dyed black and substituted for ebony.

Butternut was often called white walnut. It isn't. It is a different tree. It is lighter in weight and paler in color.

Finished sycamore is a very light brown. Stained greenish-yellow it was called harewood in England.

A panel with the wood grain running horizontally is called a landscape panel.

Thonet bentwood pieces made of beechwood were stained to look like rosewood or mahogany.

CLARIFICATIONS

A reproduction is a modern copy. With a little help they might be sold as authentic pieces.

A fake is a copy of an authentic piece made to be sold as if it were the "real thing". "Nice people" sell "unnice" pieces.

Restoration is more than simple repair. It means to renew and return a piece to its first state. New parts can be substituted for missing or damaged ones. Restoration is proper and important. Without restoration, many lovely pieces would be lost forever. Skilled craftspeople are very valuable. A major restoration is the replacement of front legs, the feet, casepiece tops, one or more drawers, reshaping a seat frame, a chair splat, the wings of an arm chair, replacing a bonnet-top, and similar work.

"Subbing" is substituting parts on an antique piece for repairs or deception.

"Subbed" or "monkeyed" means a repair or addition, such as a carved shell, for the purpose of making a piece look older or more valuable.

Market value is the retail cash value of a piece.

Check the vocabulary under "auction" for pertinent information dealing with auctions.

A "divorce" is separating a piece into two parts. This is done when they are worth more separate.

What about married pieces? Unhappily married anything is not a pleasure, but happily married furniture can be desirable. New England which "wasted not" thought so and I agree. Married pieces are not classified as fakes if properly identified. "Hasty weddings" not always work out well. Some pieces are truly "living-in-sin"!

An appraisal is the worth of a piece, valued by an expert, usually in writing, often for insurance.

AN AMERICAN FURNITURE VOCABULARY

Absentee bid   Also called a "pocket bid". This is a bid or offer left in person or by mail with an auctioneer before or prior to the auction. See "auctions".

Acanthus   A leaf design. The acanthus was a wild plant native to Southern Europe. Its beautiful ragged leaves were an important decorative detail on columns in the Classical period of Greece and Rome. The Renaissance revived this leaf design. The Puritans carved this motif on their panel chests. The Queen Anne period carved them on their chair-knees. Chippendale carved them on his front seat-rails and chair-knees. On certain Philadelphia chairs acanthus fronds flow from the shell on the center of the crest-rail to the ears. Hepplewhite carved them on the ribs of his shield-back chairs. The American Empire period gilded their design on many pieces, and carved them double as furniture feet. The American Victorian period carved them on the upper portion of various table-legs. Open high relief acanthus scrolls are also found carved on Victorian rococo sofas and chairs. This design was important on other American pieces such as silver.

Accent panel   A wood inlay of a contrasting wood usually in a geometric shape. Examples seen on Federal pieces are often of satinwood.

Acorn   An ornament resembling an acorn. Examples are found adorning Puritan chair backposts and upsidedown on William and Mary highboys pieces as drops.

Adam   Robert, 1728-1792, James, 1730-1794. English designers that created an English style after Chippendale. While not a period in America, these formal classical designs influenced George Hepplewhite and Thomas Sheraton and evidences itself in our Federal period.

Aesop's fable motifs   Such as the fox and the grapes. Seen on 18th century Philadelphia pieces.

Alabaster   Alabaster columns are found on Empire tables, often with a mirrored back. It is a granular variety of gypsum.

All original   This means a piece that has all the parts it was born with, except for very small repairs.

American country furniture   Furniture made in small rural communities of local woods, often primitive, but employing basic designs from the urban areas. Country Chippendale pieces are a fine example.

American furniture periods

Puritan period	1650-1690
William and Mary period	1690-1720
Queen Anne period	1720-1750
Chippendale period	1750-1785
Hepplewhite period	1785-1800
Sheraton period	1800-1820
Empire period	1820-1840
Victorian period	1840-1910

Amorini   The English called carved cherubs on their furniture amorini. Amorini were winged cupids or gods of love. Examples are seen on English William and Mary pieces. Not an American design.

Anthemion   This is a Greek honeysuckle motif. Examples are seen carved on Chippendale "pierced-swag" chairs and in gilt or ormalu on American Empire pieces.

Applewood   The appletree came with the early settlers from England in 1629. John Endicott an early governor of the Massachusetts Bay Colony is given credit for bringing the first trees to America. Its color is light to medium pinkish-tan, with distinctive "spilled coffee" markings. It is hard and closegrained. Beautiful country pieces were made from this wood.

Applied arm   A separate heavy curved piece of wood at the back of windsor chairs, usually Pennsylvania or Rhode Island types.

Applied cresting   A carved ornament attached to the top-rail of a chair or sofa. Examples are seen on various New York Chippendale chairs in the form of applied shells to their serpentine, (cupid bow) crest-rail.

Applied decoration A separate added piece. Examples are spindles and eggs glued on Puritan chests, shell decorations added to embellish American Queen Anne pieces, fret-work applied to Chinese Chippendale furniture, and carved gadrooning applied to Chippendale pieces.

Applied molding A molding often geometric applied to the face of furniture to create a panelled effect. Examples are seen on Puritan panel chests and William and Mary pieces.

Applique This is an additional decoration, usually applied with glue. Examples are bosses or eggs in the Puritan period. Another example is the fret designs on Chinese Chippendale pieces in the Chippendale period. Can be referred to as applied decoration.

Appraisal The worth of a piece, valued by an expert, usually in writing, often for insurance.

Apron piece A skirt. A skirt between the legs of the seat-frame of a chair or between the legs of a casepiece. Casepieces with French feet always have an apron piece with the exception of Shaker pieces. Examples are seen on Hepplewhite chests with French feet.

Arcaded back An arch back. A furniture back with an arcade design between the top-rail and the seat. Examples are seen on various English Windsors and English Sheraton chairs. Some are seen in the American Victorian period.

Arched skirt Also called an arched or arcaded apron. An apron designed with arcade shapes that may be round or pointed. Examples are seen on William and Mary mixing tables and William and Mary highboys and lowboys. They are also found on Federal casepieces.

Arched stretchers Arched stretchers are arc or hooped shaped. Examples are seen on "C" and "S" scrolled stretchers of American and English William and Mary chairs. They are also found on various English and American Windsors.

Arches Arches on furniture are usually round (Roman) or pointed (Gothic) Examples are seen carved or painted on

Puritan chests. Also on Federal and Empire glass doors of secretaries.

Architectural furniture   Furniture in which the design includes architectural characteristics such as paneling. Usually in the form of large pieces. Examples are Puritan wainscot chests and chairs, William and Mary kas pieces (wardrobes), and certain Victorian cabinets. Broken-scroll bonnet-tops in the Chippendale period are considered an architectural element while the piece itself is not. Structural corner cupboards, perhaps with a shell carved dome and fluted columns, are architectural pieces.

Arm pads   This is partial upholstery on the arms of chairs and sofas. Examples are seen on Empire and Victorian pieces.

Arm stump   This is also called an arm support. It is the vertical piece which supports the front of a chair arm. Examples are seen on Victorian open arm chairs.

Astrogel end table   A Federal work table so called because of the oval shaped ends of the top. The base is usually pillar and claw with brass paw feet and brass castors. The cabinet has a fitted tambour slide. The "astrogel" top lifts up. Some astrogel end tables have brass trumpet feet on reeded legs.

Astrogel molding   A convex bead molding often used to overlap the joining of double doors. Examples seen in the Sheraton period.

Attenuated cabriole legs   This refers to slender cabriole legs as seen on fine Queen Anne high chests of drawers.

Auction   An auction is a public sale where property goes to the highest bidder.

The auction house owns no property, it is the agent providing a service to the seller and buyer.

An absentee bid is an offer left in person or by mail with the auctioneer before the sale. The record of absentee bids is kept by the house and given the same recognition as bids made during the actual sale. The record of an absentee bid is termed "book".

A "pool" is a clutch of bidders, not necessarily dealers, who attempt to restrain or force up bidding for their personal profit.

A "ring" is a group, usually dealers, who gather together to cheat the house and the seller by keeping the bidding if possible between themselves, and keeping it low. The "ring" after acquiring said object or objects may then hold another auction among themselves to divide the goodies.

A "switch" is the substitution of a piece originally on view, for one of a lower value prior or after the sale.

A "phantom bid" is invented by the auctioneer to run the price up in the absence of a real bid.

A reserve is the lowest price agreed on by the seller and the house beneath which the article cannot be sold. The seller will take the article back if that price is not reached.

An unreserved auction means there is no reserve and the article goes to the highest bidder no matter how low the last bid is.

A "hidden reserve" is a reserve agreed upon by the seller and the house, unknown to the bidder.

The commission to the house is called a "buyers premium".

Auction tips Larger auction houses have separate departments for furniture, paintings, etc., that have an expert in charge. Each department produces catalogues and handles sales. You can write or phone an auction house requesting particular catalogues or particular sale information. There is a charge for catalogues. You can request price (digests) sheets listing what each particular piece in the sale sold for. There is also a charge for this service.

Auction viewing rooms are the best place to see, handle and learn about furniture. Treat yourself to hours of pleasure before the sale in a category you are most interested in.

Auction descriptions can be extremely fine and accurate and they can also be faulty. Always inspect the items against the description. Some mistakes are only mistakes and not evil doing, but they can foul you up.

Be sure you know what the piece you bid on looks like. Take notes when you view it. The house will allow you to handle the piece under supervision before the sale at a "viewing time". Note distinguishing marks, cracks, colors, scratches, etc.

The private collector has the edge over the dealer who must buy at a price that enables him to sell at a profit.

"As is" is an auction term meaning the article is some way damaged and will be sold in that condition.

If you cannot be present at a particular auction and are hesitant to offer an absentee bid without viewing the piece or pieces, many dealers will bid for you. They should agree to phone you after examining the object to describe the condition. Then if you wish, to bid for you up to an agreed-on price. You will pay a commission to this person in addition to the one you pay the house. Only contact dealers that handle this particular type of object and who will be attending the auction to buy for themselves. You do not want a dealer who is not familiar with the type of piece you plan to bid on.

(See page 195 for more auction tips.)

Back stool   An early name for an upholstered side chair.

Backsplash   A decorative backboard attached to a sideboard or wash stand flanking the wall, ostensibly to protect it from splashed food or water. Some have side elements like galleries. Examples on Federal sideboards featuring a scrolled backsplash with an urn finial in the center and rope turned columns.

Bail   A half-loop metal pull, usually brass, hanging down from metal plates. In America it was first used about 1700. Examples are seen on William and Mary pieces.

Baize   A woolen fabric resembling felt, usually green, found on some Empire game tables tops.

Ball and claw foot   A foot with a dragon or eagle claw holding a pearl or ball. This design originated in the Orient. Ball and claw feet appear late in the Queen Anne period and are most important in the Chippendale period both in America and England.

Ball finial Brass or gilded wood ball decoration with a spear-like projection found on Federal tall piece pediments.

Ball foot Also called an "onion foot". A boldly turned foot in the shape of a ball. Usually has a reel shaped turning above the ball. Examples are seen on American William and Mary chests.

Ball leg tip A metal, usually brass, tip found on furniture legs in the shape of a ball that fits like a mitten without a thumb.

Ball supports A large ball, often ebonized, found on the lower shaft, supporting legs of certain Federal tables. Examples on various Boston card tables.

Ball turnings Turnings of closely spaced balls. Examples are seen on Elizabethan revival pieces in the American Victorian period.

Balloon back A hoop shaped chair-back. Examples are seen on Queen Anne chair-backs and Victorian upholstered chair-backs.

Balloon seat A round balloon-shaped seat found on various Queen Anne, Sheraton and Victorian chairs.

Bamboo turnings Turnings simulating bamboo. This was achieved by ringing. Examples are seen on some types of windsor chairs made from 1780 to 1800.

Banding A band of colored inlay contrasting with the surrounding surface. Holly, maple, satinwood, ash, and birch were often used. Examples are seen on Federal pieces.

Banister back Vertical bannisters that are set or mortised into the crest and bottom rail of chairs. Examples are seen on William and Mary chairs.

Banisters Also called "balusters", they are semi-circular spindles. Examples are seen on American William and Mary chairs.

Bar-back Hepplewhite's term for an open-back sofa.

Barrel-front This usually refers to a curved corner-piece, often consisting of two parts. This piece usually takes a 34" corner and may be panneled. Examples made in Connecticut circa 1770-1780. The term barrel-front may also describe other circular casepieces.

Barrel-turned shafts Heavy round turned table shafts usually with X-frame bases are found in the Empire period. These tables were often painted black or made of rosewood and often had gilded designs.

Base The horizontal element on casepieces immediately above the feet.

Base molding Applied molding around the base of a casepiece. Examples are seen on William and Mary pieces.

Bat's wing brasses Brass handles and escutcheon plates that resemble a bat with outstretched wings. Some are chased, stamped or have punched designs. They were first seen in the William and Mary period. They were kept brightly polished to reflect firelight.

Bead molding Small semi-circular molding. Bead molding can be seen on Sheraton drawers.

Beech A wood used infrequently in America except for underframes. Seen on some early turned pieces.

Beehive feet Empire turned feet in beehive design found on casepieces from the 1830's and associated with Baltimore furniture.

Beehive finial A decorative ornament that points upward in a beehive motif associated with Baltimore furniture in the Empire period.

Bell flower A narrow cup shaped with a flaring mouth and three to five clappers (petals). These stylized, usually hanging flowers or buds of three to five petals are carved or inlaid one under the other, often dropping down vertically on the legs or on a chair splat. Sheraton and Hepplewhite pieces use this detail.

Bell-seat A rounded bell shaped seat. Examples are seen on Philadelphia Queen Anne side chairs.

John Henry Belter A New York cabinetmaker working in the rococo revival style from 1844 to 1863. His laminated, high-carved furniture is famous. More under Victorian period.

Bench-carving A piece made separately and applied. The blazes on a Chippendale tall piece are an example.

Bevel A slanting cutting away of an edge.

Bilsted See Red Gumwood.

Birch A yellow, very hard and closegrained wood that takes a high polish. Its grain is similar to maple, but heavier. The finished color is light brown to amber. It can have a curly figure. Birch was often used by country cabinetmakers in Maine and New Hampshire. Since Birch can be stained to resemble many other woods, it was substituted for stainwood in the Federal period.

Bird cage The four small vertical posts beneath the top of some tip-and-turn tables, first seen in the Queen Anne, and later in the Chippendale period. Philadelphia made exquisite tip-and-turn tables with the bird cage detail, often called "crows nest" or "cage". Certain windsors, often bamboo turned, with a flat top rail inset with two or three spindles or a geometric shape, attached to another horizontal rail into which the back spindles are set, are often called "bird cage" or "coop back" windsor, the detail between the horizontals being the cage.

Bird's eye Small brown markings resembling a bird's eye seen on various sugar or maple timbers. Sheraton mixed this maple with mahogany to achieve colorful pieces.

Blaze See Corkscrew finial.

Blind doors Solid doors, often double, that conceal small drawers or compartments. Examples on Federal casepieces. The blind doors are between the glass enclosed top shelves and the bottom portion consisting of three drawers. Hepplewhite secretaries of 1790 have this detail.

Block Design element found on various Federal and Federal revival legs at apex, often with a concentric design. Examples on many sideboards.

Block foot A foot shaped like a cube. When the foot tapers it is called a taper foot, therm or spade foot. In the Chippendale period block feet are seen on Chinese Chippendale straight legs. In the Hepplewhite period the spade foot which tapers is an important design.

Block front Construction of casepieces in which thick timbers, usually of mahogany or cherry, are cut so that the center recedes in a flattened curve while the ends curve outward in a flattened bulge. If the piece is in two separate sections only the lower section is blockfronted. Examples are seen in the Chippendale period on Newport pieces by John Goddard. On blocked pieces are blocked bracket feet, often with the inner curve coming to a point marking the transition from the horizontal to the vertical plane. The point curves into a volute detail. Blocking is an important design and a very difficult one to achieve.

Blocks Structural element used for bracing.

Blunt arrow foot A type of foot resembling an arrow most commonly seen on certain Pennsylvania Windsor chairs.

Board chest A chest constructed by nailing boards together to form a rectangular chest. Board chests are not as strong as panel chests. Nails not dowels were used on board chests. The Puritan period produced many board chests.

Boat bed American Empire piece similar to a sleigh bed with a French origin.

Bobbin turning A turning resembling a wound bobbin. This turning is seen on certain Windsor chairs.

Bolection molding A raised molding having flat edges and a raised center. Examples seen on Empire pier tables.

Bombe' Inflated or blown out shape. Bombe' pieces are also called kettle shaped. Boston excelled at making bombe' chests in the period from 1770 to the 1790's. Bracket feet on these pieces often have a matching shape and are called swelled feet.

Bonnet-top A uniquely American architectural feature! Also referred to as a hood-top or scroll-top. This term is used when the broken-arch pediment on tall casepieces covers the entire top from fore to aft, rather than a one dimensional front piece. They were first seen in the Queen Anne period on highboys. The Chippendale period also produced bonnet-tops. In a closed bonnet-top the back of the bonnet or hood is level with the broken-arch pediment. Examples of closed-bonnets are seen on various Newport pieces in the Chippendale period.

Bookend inlay Inlay resembling bookends. Seen on Federal Hepplewhite pieces.

Bootjack legs Legs of simple chests or casepieces that are formed continuations of the sides. Examples on early six-board chests.

Boss A round or egg-shaped ornament that was glued on. Examples are seen on Puritan chests. This is an applied decoration.

Boston chair A William and Mary leather chair with a simple arched crest rail and Spanish or brush feet. Brass tacks secured the leather.

Boston rocker A uniquely American piece! A high-back Windsor chair with attached rockers that was made about 1820. The seat is called a "rolling seat" because the rear upturns and the front downturns. This is an American classic made in the Empire period.

Bow-back 18th century Windsor type chair with the curved back meeting the chair seat. See "Windsors".

Bowl turnings Broader than a cup turning. Examples on William and Mary legs. Both are called trumpet turnings.

Box sofa An Empire sofa from 1830 to 1840 with vertical ends consisting of boldly carved arm supports resting on boldly carved Roman legs.

Box stretcher Stretchers that form a rectangle. These can be seen on Chinese Chippendale pieces.

Boxed ends A detail on particular Chippendale broken pediment tall pieces. They have architectural squared ends over the lower curve of the pediment, usually with a plinth and finial in the same design as the center finial (often urn and blaze).

The box end is in line with the outer edge of the casepiece while the broken pediment extends slightly out in a concave curve. Examples on Rhode Island chest-on-chest pieces 1765 to 1790.

Braced back   This refers to Windsor chairs with two reinforcement spindles that project up from an extension behind the seat.

Bracelet   Also called a collar, cuff or wrister. These are ornamental carved or applied pieces resembling bracelets, that appear on the ankles of certain cabriole legs, terminating in Spanish feet. Examples may be seen in the American William and Mary period, often on dressing tables. Also found on English William and Mary pieces.

Bracket   Reinforcement of the angle between parts or surfaces on a piece of furniture. A shaped bracket reinforces the joining of a leg to the seat-rail of a chair. Pierced brackets are a design element of Chippendale furniture.

Bracket foot   A foot supporting a casepiece that is attached directly to the underframing. A bracket foot can be plain, scrolled or molded. Bracket feet can be seen on Chippendale desks. A bracket foot on a bombe' piece will outcurve to repeat the "kettle shape". These bracket feet are called "swelled feet".

Brad   Tiny nail that has little or no head, one usually of brass. They are one inch or shorter. Used to attach applied moldings or brasses. Brads are seen on William and Mary brass mounts.

Brass ball finial   Ball finial with spear-like projection found on the pediments of Federal tall pieces like secretaries.

Brass furniture   Term used by colonial and English merchants to describe furniture brasses and decorative furniture ornaments.

Brass inlay   Designs like rosettes, stars, anthemion, and thin strips, made of brass, set into furniture. Examples are found in the Federal period on klismos type chairs of 1815.

Brass shoe   A fitted brass foot terminating in a button. Examples are found on various Sheraton casepieces with turned legs.

Brass tacks   Also called brass studs. Seen on William and Mary leather chairs, late Chippendale chair seats, and Hepplewhite chair seats. May be placed to resemble fret work.

Breadboard ends   These are wood strips matching the tabletop in width and thickness and fastened to the top with wooden pins or hand-forged nails. They protected the table ends from damage. Many country tables have this feature.

Breakfast table   A small table with hinged side leaves. Originally intended for one person. They were first seen in the Queen Anne period. Pembroke, and handkerchief tables are referred to as "breakfast tables".

Broken arch pediment   Pediment broken in arch shape. Also called goose-neck, swan-neck, or scroll top. Examples are seen on Chippendale tall pieces. A swan-neck is the most vertical type.

Broken pediment   A pediment (a pointed or curved piece used above the cornice on tall casepieces) with the moldings broken at the center for ornamental purposes. These were first seen in America in the Queen Anne period on highboys. Greek and Roman temples were the origin.

Brush foot   A Spanish foot that does not curve under. Examples in the William and Mary period.

Buffet   French word describing antique sideboards. It is also used to describe open doorless furniture of more than one tier.

Bun foot   Foot, perhaps of Dutch origin, shaped like a flattened bun. A form of English bun foot is called a "melon foot". The English melon foot has vertical grooves while the American bun foot does not. Bun feet are seen on many American and English William and Mary pieces.

Bureau   In England, a desk, but in America a chest of drawers. For example, Sheraton chests are called bureaus.

Bureau table   A kneehole desk or kneehole chest of drawers. These are characterized by a single wide top drawer and tiers of narrow lower drawers flanking an opening that has a cupboard in back. Examples, 1750 to 1790, were produced in Massachusetts, Newport, New York and Pennsylvania.

Burl veneer   The growth (burl) from a tree trunk sliced for veneer. Antique veneer is thicker than new veneer. Burl veneer is found on American and English William and Mary pieces.

Bust finial   A sculptured representation of the upper part of the human figure including the head, neck and part of the shoulders and breast found on the center plinth as a finial on certain high chests and secretaries in the Chippendale period. Examples are found on various Philadelphia pieces. The bust may be wood carved or porcelain. If the bust is of a buxom lady with draped breasts it may be a "Pompadour" finial after Madame Pompadour. The pieces they appear on are sometimes called "Pompadour chests."

Butterfly hinge   The earliest hinge used in America. It is shaped like a bow-tie. Seen on Puritan and William and Mary pieces.

Butterfly table   An early table with swinging leaf brackets, that can be round, oval, or rectangular. They have turned legs and are about 22 to 28 inches tall. They may have a drawer with a wooden knob. These tables are rare and valuable. American butterfly tables appear in the Puritan period and in the William and Mary period. Butterfly tables with the wings pivoted into the stretchers are believed to be uniquely American.

Butternut   A hard and closegrained wood that takes a good finish. It is a light brown when finished. Butternut is sometimes called white walnut, but it is not the same tree. Butternut is paler than the lightest northern walnut. It is also lighter in weight than any true walnut. Butternut is often found on country casepieces. During the Victorian period butternut was stained to resemble black walnut.

Button feet   Feet shaped like a button are seen on cabriole legs of small pieces such as tripod candlesticks from 1730 to 1750. Also many turned chair legs had button feet.

Buttons   A turned circular design detail found on certain Sheraton chairs on the legs and stiles. This detail was applied. Examples on some klismos type chairs about 1805.

Buyers premium   Surcharge added to the purchase of auction lots. (See auction points.)

"C" scroll A single convolute. Examples on William and Mary cane-chairs and daybeds and upholstered arms of easy chairs. Also on various cabriole legs on the inside of the cabriole. Certain Rococo Revival couches had "C" scroll legs. Mid-nineteenth "balloon-back" side chairs had pierced "C" scrolls on the horizontal splat.

Cabochons Raised oval ornaments that were used as decorations. They were also called jewels. Chippendale chairs made in Philadelphia during the Chippendale period sometimes had small cabochons at the knee. Cabochons were seen more often on English pieces and they were usually larger.

Cabriole chair Hepplewhite's word to describe his upholstered chairs. They do not have cabriole legs, but tapered ones.

Cabriole leg Also called a "crooked leg". It is a leg that curves outward at the knee and inward towards the foot in an elongated "S" shape. This leg is Oriental in origin. The cabriole leg is first seen late in the William and Mary period in America. It assumes more importance in the Queen Anne period and in the Chippendale period.

Cabriole sofa A Federal Hepplewhite piece. It does not have cabriole legs, but eight tapered inlaid legs, shaped arms, and is of curvilinear form. The curve from the back to the arms is beautiful.

Cage work Any detail that resembles a cage. An example is the "bird-cage", four small vertical posts beneath the top of certain Chippendale tip-and-turn tables. Sometimes called a "crows nest". Also called a "coop" detail on various windsor pieces with a geometric cage shape or shapes beneath the top rail.

Camel back A furniture back with a convex in the center, resembling a camel. Another descriptive name is "serpentine back". Examples are seen on various American and English Chippendale sofas.

Candle-brackets Also called "candle-slides". Small sliding platforms built into a casepiece to hold a candlestick. These are often seen on American and English Queen Anne pieces.

Candle drawers   Narrow vertical drawers found on either side of the central locker in the interior of various slant-front desks. Examples on Pennsylvania Queen Anne slant-top desks circa 1740.

Cane   Cane was made from stems of palms or grasses that were woven into a mesh. Originated in the Orient as a furniture material. William and Mary chairs had caning. Some Sheraton sofas were caned on the seat as well as the back. Also seen on various Empire chair seats. Cane was used on English pieces also.

Canted   Shape resulting when the corners of a square are cut off. The canted portion is often reeded or fluted. This detail may be seen on many Chippendale desks and chests.

Capital   Projecting piece at the top of a column or pillar. Capitals may be seen on certain Empire tables that have pillars or columns. Lotus capitals are seen on Egyptian designs in the Victorian period.

Capstan table   A drum table, usually with drawers or shelves in the skirt. Has a pedestal and outcurved legs. Examples in the Federal period.

Carcase   The body of a casepiece. It does not include drawers or doors. It is like a turkey without wings, legs, head or tail.

Card table   Also called a "gaming" or "game table", a folding table used for games. Some card or game tables have concave saucers called guinea pockets or scoops for chips. These tables might also have outsquared or outrounded corners for candles. Game tables are first seen in the Queen Anne period.

Carrying handles   Usually of brass, these handles were on either side of a casepiece to facilitate moving the piece. Examples are seen in the Chippendale period. Many bombe' chests have carrying handles.

Cartouche   A scroll design. It was used on the central finial of certain Philadelphia Chippendale highboys. This design was also seen on many Victorian pieces, on chair and sofa top-rails.

Cartouche-back   A chair or sofa back shaped like a cartouche or scroll. Examples are seen on American Victorian Renaissance revival furniture.

Caryatids   These are carved female figures. Examples may be seen on American Empire columns. Similar male figures are called Atlantes. Types with a male bearded turbaned head are known as "Turks Heads" or "mummy headed therms" and are found on American Empire furniture from Baltimore and Philadelphia.

Castor   Small wheel on a swivel attached to furniture legs. Many American Victorian chairs have castors.

Cat's paw feet   A foot resembling a cat's paw. A Newport Rhode Island detail found on stands between 1765 and 1792.

Cavetto cornice   A concave shaped cornice. Examples on Queen Anne highboys some of which were designed with removable bonnet type tops.

Cellerette drawers   End sections of Federal sideboards, often curved, with several divisions, and often lead lined, for storage of wine bottles.

Central locker   This is the storage part in the center of the interior of a slant or slope front desk, with the document drawers on either side. Many lockers have secret hiding places behind them. Gold coins were often hidden in the secret place. Also called a prospect door. Examples in Queen Anne and Chippendale periods.

Chair seats   Chair seats are approximately 16 to 18 inches from the floor on American chairs. Victorian rockers may be 12 to 14 inches from the floor.

Chair table   A chair with a solid back that swings down on the arms of the chair to form a table. Made in America beginning in the 17th century.

Chamfered   A shaped bevelled edge usually at a 45 angle. Examples are seen on Chippendale casepieces. Chamfered edges may be fluted, stop-fluted, or reeded.

Channel molding   Grooved molding. Examples may be seen on Puritan pieces.

Chasing A type of engraving. Early chasing was done with a pointed metal tool. Chasing is seen on early American brass mounts made in the William and Mary period on teardrop and Bat's wing brasses.

Cherry wood American black or wild cherry grows all through the eastern half of America, except in southern Florida. It is reddish-brown. This wood is moderately hard and is straight grained. On various timbers a simple ring-growth figure can be found. On rare occasions swirl, feather, or wavy figures are evident. The texture of cherry is fine with small pores. During colonial times, black cherry was used in the states north of Pennsylvania and New Jersey. In New England and New York cherry was used to make some of the finest pieces including highboys, lowboys, secretaries and chests. Cherry was combined with maple in the Federal periods.

Chest Box with a hinged lid. Drawers were added later in the 17th century.

Chestnut wood The chestnut tree grew in North America from Southern Maine to Delaware and Ohio and Southern Illinois. Wood used for drawers and hidden parts, and for backboards. On occasion it is seen on country pieces such as 18th century chests. It is a yellowish-brown when finished. There is a resemblance to oak.

Chest-on-a-chest Chest of drawers in two parts. A double chest. These are often seen in the Chippendale period.

Chest-on-a-frame Raised chest on a frame with legs under it. These pieces are seen first in the Puritan period.

Chinese Chippendale Chippendale style using Chinese or quasi-Chinese designs. Chinese Chippendale pieces are found in the American Chippendale period. (More information on Chinese Chippendale found under "Chippendale")

Chinoiserie 18th century style of decoration in which supposedly Chinese motifs were used. This form of decoration climaxed about 1750. This fanciful decoration is first seen in America in the William and Mary period on japanned pieces. (More information in William and Mary period)

45

Chip carving   A simple low relief form of carving executed with flat chisels, and gouges, usually in geometric patterns. This type of carving was done in the Puritan period. It is also found late in the Victorian period.

Chippendale   Thomas Chippendale (1718-1779) - An English designer in the Georgian period.

Chippendale period   American Chippendale Furniture 1750-1785 (English 1705-1779)

Operative Words: mahogany, Chinese, French, rococo, lavish, block and shell, cupids bow, ball and claw foot

Our glorious Chippendale period is named for the great Georgian designer Thomas Chippendale. He was born in 1718 in Worcester, Otley, or London, England depending on what biography you read. We do know he was in London in 1749, and published a book of his furniture designs in 1754. This book titled "The Director" did indeed direct. He was also the author of "The Cabinetmaker Directory". Chippendale was a superb carver and this ability is reflected in his work. The period predates the Revolutionary War. After the war the Federal style Hepplewhite period commenced.

The term Chippendale style includes designs that were known and employed previously. Chippendale incorporating many influences was basically embellishing Queen Anne designs. In America from 1750 to 1785 furniture in the Chippendale style was primarily of mahogany. This grand, impressive period was the most elaborate and luxurious seen in America up to this time. This is perhaps our finest furniture hour. Between 1760 and 1776 craftsmen in Newport, Rhode Island fashioned singularly beautiful block and shell pieces. Equally exquisite furniture was produced in Philadelphia. It is interesting to note that the Quakers were responsible for this lavish Philadelphia furniture.

This period is a further development of the Queen Anne style with Chinese and French rococo additions and salted with a dash of Gothic. Chippendale, the designer, started with

Dutch styles and moved towards the French and Chinese. This resulted in both curved and straight lines seen on Chippendale pieces. The Chinese influence is seen in the square, untapering legs and later in delicate open work called fret work. These pieces are called "Chinese Chippendale". English pieces in the Chinese style might have pagoda tops and might be gilded. American Chippendale is less square than the English and has simpler carving. English Chippendale is usually larger and more complex. Another Chinese influence is seen in the ball and claw foot on cabriole legs. In the Orient this foot symbolized a dragon and pearl.

American Chippendale furniture is seldom as ornate as its English counterpart. English and American ornamentation included gilding and carving. American pieces have less of both ornamentation. American chairs are narrower than English ones and less square. Nevertheless, many English chairs were simple and can pass for Massachusetts Chippendale. These usually have pudgy claws and no stretchers.

American Queen Anne hoop or yoke back chairs with curved top-rails and Dutch feet were replaced with the Chippendale chair which had serpentine top-rails called "cupid bows" with Chinese influenced "ears". The "ears" are turned up extremities of the top-rail, and when they are carved in a spiral they are said to be voluted. Chippendale cabriole legs were heavier than the Queen Anne types. He used the claw and ball foot first seen late in the Queen Anne period.

Chippendale replaced the solid Queen Anne splat with pierced carved splats. These had designs of arches, ruffles, loops, heart designs, reverse curves, diamonds, ribbons, and tassels. Pendant husks, trefoils, quatrefoils, and Chinese lattice were also used for the splat. The cabriole leg with a claw and ball foot was used on the open splat chair.

The open-work splat on Chippendale chairs had a French origin. A perfect example is the English Chippendale ribbon-back chair, with cabriole legs, terminating in a French whorl or scroll foot. The ribbon-back was never made in America, but people think of it whenever "Chippendale chair" is mentioned. Perhaps because it is pictured widely in furniture books. A much simpler ribbon design chair-splat was made in New York, Pennsylvania and Maryland.

In some instances the ball on the claw and ball foot is simply a half ball, cut on the bottom to produce a flat surface to stand on. Claw and ball feet were used only on the front legs. The back legs were straight, square, or rounded, with a slight slant called a rake, and end in a footless or stump conclusion. The straight "Marlbough" type leg found on Chinese Chippendale pieces usually had straight stretchers. These legs might be reeded or fluted like the "pretzel-back" and "pierced swag-back" chairs. English Chinese Chippendale chairs may be seen with cabriole front legs terminating in a claw and ball foot.

Chippendale used Gothic pointed arch shapes on a variety of pieces like cabinets, bookcases and chairs. As a rule Chippendale chairs had no carving on the back. Most pre-Revolutionary chairs were based on English examples, not on design books. After the war, source books had a more direct influence on American furniture.

American Chippendale furniture was decorated with elaborate shell, scrolls, foliage, gadroon carving, acanthus leaves, and Chinese fretwork. Inlay was no longer popular, and rarely ordered. Japanned decoration in red, green, and gilt is often used on a blue-green background. Black and brown were also ground colors. English pieces were designed with vermillion and green grounds as well as black and brown. The gilding is raised and heavy on English pieces. English pieces with "Chinese taste" added dragons and long-tailed birds. American jappaning is thiner. Designs for jappaned pieces came from design books as well as Oriental plates. Fine pieces were made in Boston, Philadelphia and New York.

Chippendale seat-frames were straight on all four sides. Sometimes the seat-rail was decorated with a carved shell. Some Philadelphia seat-rails are heavily carved on the front and have ornately carved front cabriole legs. On rare occasion a ruffled shell overlaps the seat frame on New York chairs. This trait is not rare on English chairs. On Philadelphia seat-rails, gadrooning or acanthus carving can be seen. Fret-work was often applied on "Chinese Chippendale" seat-rails. The lower edge of Chippendale seat-rails is straight. The seat was known as a "slip-seat" because it could be slipped or lifted out of the frame.

The arms outcurve and end in voluted scrolls or carved knuckles. They are supported by arm-stumps.

Walnut chairs were usually not veneered. Side chairs are about 40 inches high.

Philadelphia was said to have produced the finest pierced splat chair. These favored rococo or Gothic shapes and the French scrolled toe might appear on their cabriole legs. The carving is very fine.

Massachusetts was known for slender pieces and for that reason used a block and spindle stretcher on their chairs to strengthen them. New York favored the tassel, ruffle or diamond surrounded by strapwork for their splats. New York chairs sometimes upholstered their seats over the seat-rail. Newport used an oval ball for their claw and ball feet. Connecticut often stained their cherry wood to imitate mahogany. The Salem area produced chairs with an undulating crest-rail that flows into the top of the stiles. Rhode Island favored a cross-hatched crest rail.

Another type of Chippendale chair had horizontal parallel bars or ladder-splats and was called the "pretzel-back". The pretzel-back had straight legs and a box-stretcher. The straight legs might be reeded or fluted. The arms if present are slightly outcurved. A variation was the pierced swag chair also called a "trotter-type" for cabinetmaker Daniel Trotter of Philadelphia. It had a pierced swag crest-rail and horizontal pierced swag slats, often with a honeysuckle design in an oval at the center of each splat and the crest-rail.

English hoop-back chairs in the Queen Anne style continued to be produced into the 1780's and were covered with carved tracery. On some English chairs dolphin feet were substituted for claw and ball feet. English seat-rails were often ornately carved, leading to ornately carved cabriole legs, perhaps terminating in outcurving or incurving scroll feet.

English Chinese Chippendale chairs could also be extremely complex with pagoda crest-rails and triple-cluster column legs. English hoop-back arm chairs with straight Chinese style unstretchered legs could have a back composed of Gothic arches. Carved swags are often seen on English seat-rails.

The Chippendale lowboys had a new feature. This was a carved or fret-work edge under the top. Their cabriole legs end in large claw and ball feet. The knees are carved with shell or foliage designs. The skirt is also carved. Philadelphia skirts are deep. The oblong tops are 32 to 36 inches wide with a molded edge. The top overhangs the piece about three inches at the ends and about two inches at the front. There is often a long drawer above three narrower ones. The center bottom drawer and the apron center usually have a fan carving. Pennsylvania lowboys were made of curly maple with Spanish feet and also were made of mahogany and walnut early in the period. These early pieces resemble William and Mary furniture.

French designs also influenced Chippendale's casepieces. These English casepieces were often very elaborate with richly carved details, more rococo lines, and generally appear fancier than American Chippendale pieces.

Chippendale referred to his upholstered side-chairs as "French chairs". Upholstered side chairs made for the southern states would have expensive material on the front and inexpensive fabric on the back as only servants (slaves) could see the backs.

Chippendale also designed upholstered "Martha Washington" type easy chairs (arm chair) with square or cupid's bow top-rail, sometimes with fret-work on the arms, legs, and stretchers. The English parallel was the "Gainsborough chair", named for the artist who painted many of his subjects seated in this type of chair.

Many English Chippendale arm chairs have extremely ornate aprons, arm-stumps, and handholds. Some have scroll and leaf carved feet. English chairs are usually larger than American chairs.

The American Chippendale wing-chair had serpentine backs, cabriole or straight legs and rolled arms. They are larger than American Queen Anne wing-chairs. Philadelphia wing-chairs could be very elaborately carved. Some even had masks carved on their aprons. American Chippendale wing-chairs were also made as rocking chairs late in the period.

American Windsor chairs do not usually have cabriole legs, (some were made in Philadelphia) but English Windsors often have them. American Windsors have backs composed of spindles. English Windsors often use backs made up of Gothic arches and open work splats. In the American Chippendale period Windsors were made with low-backs, comb-backs, bow-backs, loop-backs, fan-backs, and cage or coop-backs.

The sofa as we know it appeared in the Chippendale period. The Queen Anne period had upholstered settees and a few upholstered sofas. The sofas resembled an upholstered chair whose width had been doubled or even tripled. Early Chippendale sofas had a longer seat and a lower back than Queen Anne pieces. Later Chippendale sofas had backs of serpentine curves and roll-over arms. The sofa backs followed the line of the chair backs. These high curved backs were called camel-humps or camel-backs and were about 36 inches high. This piece was supported by six or eight legs.

The sofas with eight legs had plain square Marlborough legs; the rear legs were usually slanted and braced with a box stretcher that was three or four inches from the floor and set back, so not to bump the ankles. The six legged sofa had cabriole legs in the front, ending in claw and ball feet with knees decorated with scroll, shell, or foliage carving and plain slanted rear legs. The largest were made in Philadelphia. Double chairs or love seats and daybeds continued to be made in the Chippendale period.

The Philadelphia style Chippendale highboys and lowboys are considered to be some of the finest American pieces ever made. They are from 7-1/2 feet to 8 feet high. They are usually of crotch-grain mahogany veneer. The center drawer on the lower portion was often decorated with a carved fan or shell design. The deep apron or skirt is cut in cyma curves often with a carved design in the center. On Philadelphia pieces the entire apron might be carved but this is not usual on other Chippendale highboys. The cabriole legs on these pieces are a little shorter and the knees are beautifully carved. The balls in the claw and ball feet are almost round. The front corners of the lower part as well as the corners on the upper section often have fluted columns. The top part of the highboy is about 41 to 46 inches wide. These pieces have bonnet tops. The inner ends of the bonnet-scrolls terminate with carved flowers, leaves, large pierced cabochons, or flower baskets, that are carved separately and applied. The scrolls have square molded plinths at their outer corners decorated with carvings of flames (also called blazes and corkscrews) rising out of turned urn finials. They may also have a turned urn finial with flames in the center of the bonnet where the pediment is broken. A carved frieze is centered under the bonnet and on the lower portion at the center above the apron. There usually are nine drawers in the top and three in the lower portion. It has been said that Philadelphia highboys had the same milliner as Irish tall pieces.

The other colonies made highboys too, but Philadelphia made the most spectacular ones. The bonnet-top was also made outside of Philadelphia. Fine bonnet-top highboys were made in Connecticut and Rhode Island. New England highboys have plain scrolled bonnets with a rosette or simple flame or urn finial in the center of the pediment. These were about 46 inches wide and 7 to 9 feet high. The skirts are valanced, often in three arches. The central drawer in the upper and lower part are often fan-carved. The top part may have fluted columns while the lower may not. The legs are cabriole with claw and ball feet.

The Chippendale period also made flat-top highboys with 12 drawers that were 44 to 46 inches wide and 5-1/2 feet to 6 feet 9 inches tall. They were made in maple, cherry, and walnut as well as mahogany, and might have carving at the knees.

Newport made their highboys with closed bonnet-tops, often with only one double-tiered finial in the center. Pediments instead of solid bonnets are seen on some highboys, often with lattice-work combined with the scrolled pediments.

Tall casepieces other than highboys had broken pediment tops or bonnets that were more ornate than earlier Queen Anne pieces. Some were plain and some were fretted. Fretted pediment tops are often seen on Philadelphia double chests. Tall or double chests often had decorated friezes and cornices. Their English counterparts were usually more ornately decorated. The finials topping tall casepieces such as secretaries were in the shape of urns, eagles, flames (blazes, corkscrews), busts, and extremely stylized birds. Casepieces might have reeded pilasters, and candlestick slides were usual. Secretaries were 38 to 46 inches wide and 7 to 8 feet high. English secretaries usually have glass cupboard doors while American cupboard doors usually are solid paneled wood. However, since furniture was custom made, glass doors are sometimes seen on American pieces.

English tall casepieces might have bookcase tops with large ovals of glass, elaborate carving of ribbons or foliage, topped with carved pediments with finials. The bottom part would repeat the oval design on solid doors with the use of molding and carving. Tall English casepieces in the Chinese style were made of figured mahogany and often gilded. American tall chests with graduated drawers, often had quarter-round reeded pilasters and bracket feet.

Double chests or chest-on-chest pieces were popular in the Chippendale period. Many had bonnets or pediments. Fans and pinwheels appear on these pieces. They have bracket, ogee bracket, or short cabriole legs with a Dutch foot or blocked ogee bracket feet.

Cabinet pieces with curved fronts appeared, taking several forms. One is the serpentine curved front. Another is the oxbow, the reverse of the serpentine in that it goes inward at the center and out at the handles and then makes a return inward and straightens out at the corners. A third type is the bombe' or kettle-shaped chest. Boston cabinetmakers perfected Dutch style bombe' chests. Bombe' pieces include chests, desks, and desks with bookcases, and were made between 1770 and 1790. Bombe' pieces are seldom English. Large bombe' casepieces often have side brass handles. Casepieces continue to have bracket feet with double cyma or ogee curves.

The corners of the Chippendale chests of drawers were sometimes chamfered or beveled and were fluted or carved on this beveled edge. Most chest corners, however, were plain. The ogee bracket foot was used on desks, secretaries and chests.

English serpentine chests were often rococo and ornate with heavily carved beveled edges and extremely large and ornate brasses. American desks were generally mahogany or cherry; English ones were often walnut, yew, amboyna veneer with elaborate inlay, perhaps of human figures on the interior doors. Slant top desks in America and England often had secret compartments behind the central locker for gold coins.

The drawers on casepieces were usually constructed with a very thin molding on the edge, which is called a lip-edge or over-lapping molding because when closed, the drawer fits flush with the molding overlapping. Later just before the Hepplewhite period a beaded edge appears.

Few tables in the Queen Anne period and in the Chippendale period can be identified exclusively as dining tables. The tables which appear to be dining tables have drop leaves, but they may have been used in other rooms also. I did not find designs of dining tables in cabinetmaker's design books during this period. Chippendale drop-leaves have oval or rectangular tops often with a drawer, six to eight cabriole legs with claw and ball feet are usual. The knees are often carved. The tables are from 4 to 7 feet long.

Cabriole or straight legs were used on tables. Cabriole legs with baluster turnings above are English. Tripod tables, some with lovely carving on the pedestal and legs, often with snake or slipper feet, were very much in style. Tripod tables became a definite fashion in the Chippendale period, although they had been seen since as early as 1670 in America. They had been seen in Holland since 1650. Chippendale tripods have upturned feet while Hepplewhite tripods will have tapered toes. The stems or pillars or shaft of the English and American tripod styles are quite alike, a shaft, above, perhaps with a leaf-carved vase, ending with the tripod itself. The tripod pie-crust table has an edge made up of ogee's and scrolls, similar to rims on large English salvers that took their shape from Chinese dishes. Chippendale pie-crust tables with the entire tray carved like a Chinese dish are always English. The tripod tilt-top table sitting on a "bird cage" in pillar-and-claw style was a late addition and is considered an important Chippendale piece.

Pembroke tables were made in the Chinese Chippendale style with cross diagonal stretchers. Tea tables are rectangular and circular.

Oblong side tables were made with red veined marble tops. Side tables, especially those from Philadelphia, could be rather ornate with gadroon carving on the apron edge, carving on the sides, and carving on the cabriole legs, ending in claw and ball feet. Philadelphia side tables are seen with an upturned whorl foot resting on a shell.

English side tables might have upturned whorl feet resting on oval turnings that look like a vertical egg. Large English tables were made with red veined marble tops.

Card or gaming tables had tops formed of two leaves. The leaves were hinged. These tables are 32 to 40 inches wide. The corners are out-rounded or out-squared for candlesticks and often have four guinea pockets. They have four or five feet tall, slender cabriole legs. The claw and ball feet are on the large side and were sometimes made in a square form. Carving is often seen on the knees of the cabriole legs.

New York gaming tables have the fifth leg and a serpentine frame. In Connecticut the tables have the claw and ball front foot with the ball made like a vertical egg, and the back legs in a Dutch pad foot. Philadelphia tables usually have guinea pockets as well as turreted corners for candlesticks. Fifth legs if present are attached to a swinging bracket.

Some gaming tables have a small drawer. Various tables have Marlborough legs and Chinese type fret-work for decorations. Gadrooning decorated New York and Philadelphia pieces. Massachusetts turreted their tops for teacups as well as candlesticks which made them very decorative. Philadelphia tables are usually mahogany. Many New England tables are cherry or walnut. Maple was used in New England and New Hampshire. Various game tables have "let-in tops". This is an expensive detail. The top is slightly recessed (dished) to accommodate velvet, needlework or leather, allowing it to lay flush with the surrounding wood area. The top "lets-in" the additional material.

Newport created America's most original fine furniture. Some of the most important pieces of American furniture were made by John Goddard and Job Townsend, both Quakers from Newport, Rhode Island. These two, father and son-in-law, and William Savery of Philadelphia, made block front and shell carved casepieces. These are important, not only because of their beauty, but also because they were American designs and were said to have been unique to America. (This is not entirely true as blocking is found on French, Scandinavian, German and Italian pieces and also on Chinese export furniture. Blocking is not, however, an English characteristic). Thomas Chippendale made no designs of block-front pieces. It is believed this style in American originated in Boston, Massachusetts in the second quarter of the 18th century, and later acquired a Chippendale nature. Block front pieces were made in Massachusetts, Connecticut and New York. They are highly valued, highly priced and very beautiful. Chippendale block and shell pieces bring the stunning simplicity of Queen Anne to mind. They are an important American symbol of beauty and craftsmanship.

Block front pieces are cut from solid wood without veneering. Heavy cuban mahogany was the most practicable wood for this   purpose. Cherry was also used on block type pieces. The center front of a block-front casepiece recedes in a shallow concave curve between slightly convex ends. Blocking is achieved by shaping one timber, six or seven inches thick, or making separate blocks which was quicker and easier.

Block front pieces are often referred to as block-and-shell

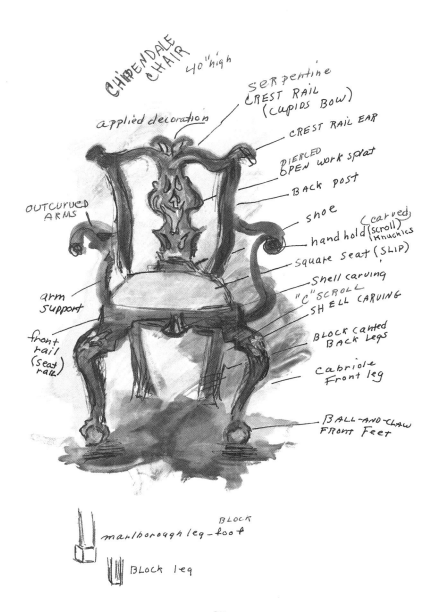

CHIPENDALE CHAIR 40" high

serpentine CREST RAIL (CUPIDS BOW)

applied decoration

CREST RAIL EAR

PIERCED OPEN work splat

BACK post

OUTCURVED ARMS

shoe

hand hold (carved) (scroll) knuckles

square seat (SLIP)

Shell carving

"C" SCROLL SHELL CARVING

arm support

BLOCK canted BACK Legs

front rail (seat rail)

cabriole Front leg

BALL-AND-CLAW FRONT Feet

marlborough leg-foot BLOCK

BLOCK leg

57

Reverse-curve back

OUTSCROLLED
arms

Camel-
Back

upholstery
covers
frame

straight legs

STRETCHER

about 6" high

Chippendale Six-Leg Sofa
Straight Fluted legs
Stretcher Quarter Way Back

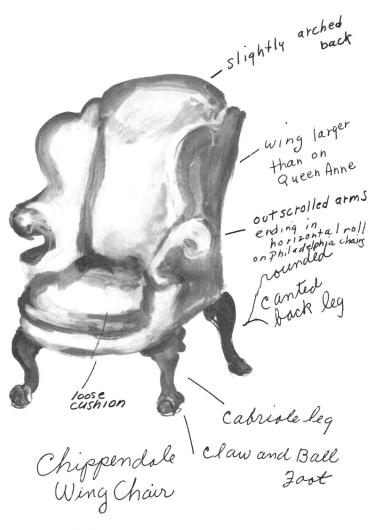

slightly arched back

wing larger than on Queen Anne

outscrolled arms ending in horizontal roll on Philadelphia chairs

rounded
canted back leg

loose cushion

cabriole leg

claw and Ball Foot

Chippendale Wing Chair

Could have a Marlborough leg and blocked foot and stretchers.

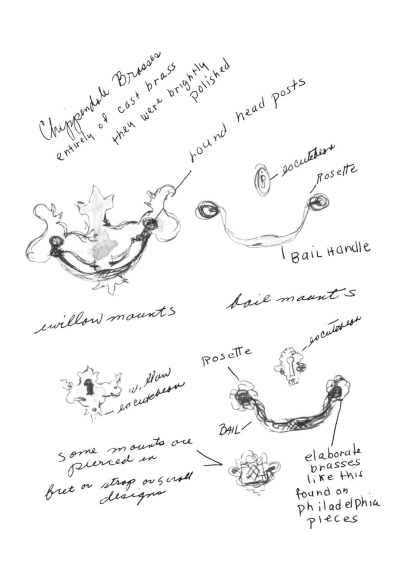

Chippendale Brasses
entirely of cast brass
they were brightly
polished

round head posts

escutcheon

Rosette

BAIL Handle

willow mounts

bail mounts

escutcheon

willow
escutcheon

Rosette

BAIL

Some mounts are
pierced in
fret or strap or scroll
designs

elaborate
brasses
like this
found on
Philadelphia
pieces

pieces because most have shell carving. On a chest of drawers, shell carving is above the top drawers and on the top or upper parts of the casepieces, below the bonnet. if the piece is in two separate sections, sometimes only the lower portion is block fronted. The tray tops of block and shell chests of drawers have their molding worked from the solid board of the top.

On block-front slant top desks there may be no carving, but if there is, it will be shell carving. Shell carving is seen on the slant lid at the top and inside the desk above the pigeon holes and document drawers. There are two types of Goddard-Townsend knee hole desks; one decorated with three carved shells and another with four carved shells. They are about 33 inches high.

Shell carving is not usual on the bottom of a casepiece, but is seen on some secretaries on the apron above the legs directly in the center. Block pieces have bracket feet as well as claw and ball feet.

Tall block casepieces have broken pediments or flat tops. Pieces with broken pediments have finials of rosettes and fluted urns with flames called blazes or corkscrews emerging from them. The top sections have solid wooden doors, often with shell carving. On very important secretaries with broken pediments, raised panels are seen under the scroll top.

The block front pieces were mainly of mahogany or cherry. The brasses on them are the willow type. The new State Department rooms in Washington, D.C. have beautiful Chippendale furniture and some spectacular block-front pieces.

(Mounts) The handles on Chippendale furniture were willow brasses with bails or rosettes on bails. Some willow plates are pierced with intricate fretwork, strap, or scroll patterns. Block front pieces often have larger willow plates than usual. Chippendale escutcheons match the plates and use three nails, one at the bottom and at the sides. Chippendale brasses have beveled edges which were cleaned by filing. These brasses are cast, not stamped. They are thin and light yellow in color.

English brasses made for the English market were often larger and more ornate than those used on American furniture. Modern companies copy the antique ones with success. It is safe to be in the doubtful column when looking at brasses. The brasses were kept brightly polished to add counter points of light to rooms by reflecting the fire and candlelights.

Forgeries of Chippendale labels of William Savery and James Gillingham keep appearing. Check for man-made aging or wormholes on labels. Look out for old newspapers (accidentally(?) left in drawers).

(Famous Chippendale cabinetmakers) Some famous furniture makers in the American Chippendale period include John Goddard, John Townsend, Gilbert Ash, John Bachman, Benjamin Burnham, Aaron Chapin, Eliphalet Chapin, Dunlap Family, Thomas Elfe, John Elliott, John Folwell, Benjamin Frothingham, James Gillingham, Jonathan Gostelowe, Adam Hains, Joseph Hosmer, Benjamin Randolph, William Savery and Thomas Tufft.

(Woods) The Chippendale period used mahogany, cherry and walnut as its principal woods. Mahogany is the most important wood in this period. It is called the perfect cabinet wood because of the diameter of mahogany trees. Table leaves made of this wood are practically always of one piece. Mahogany is a tropical wood of great strength and firm texture with a variety of grains and figures. The color range is from a deep reddish-brown to yellowish or pinkish tones. This fine wood comes from Honduras and the West Indian Islands, Jamaica, Puerto Rico, Cuba and Santo Domingo. The heartwood of mahogany possesses a capacity for repelling larvae that damage furniture woods. Marked timbers display stripe, mottle effects, curl, blister, roe and plum-pudding markings and fine fiddle-back figures. Mahogany does not gray from sunlight. This is a wood that could be beautifully carved and does not appreciably shrink and warps less than any other wood.

Mahogany from the West Indies is the important wood of this period, but walnut was used on many early pieces and cherry was used in New England. Walnut was called butternut in some areas, but should not have been so described. Butternut is a different wood which is characterized by large pores and is paler in color than the lightest northern walnut and is softer and lighter in weight than any true walnut. It is also a weaker timber, but it is easily worked and takes a good finish.

Cherry (black) is moderately hard and straight grained. It is reddish-brown when finished with a color that approaches that of mahogany. On some timbers, a mild type of ring growth figure can be found and in rare instances, swirl, feather-crotch or wavy figures are seen on choice pieces. The texture is fine with small pores.

Walnut is moderately hard and also can withstand the furniture beetle, which English walnut could not. It is characterized by a light brown or grayish brown color that will gray from exposure to sunlight. American walnut is more difficult to work than the European. This timber has a handsome grain and may show markings of stripes, waves, and mottled figures.

Maple - Rock or sugar maple was the specie most used for furniture in America. It is strong and hard and has a straight grain.

The English style following Chippendale was known as "Adam", but this style was never popular in America. The reason is that Adam's designs were never published, and this furniture was made primarily for rich Englishmen, and not for export. After the Revolutionary War, the Adam period was over. However, we will see the influence of the Adam brothers in the Hepplewhite period and in the Sheraton period.

Classic period Ancient Greece and Rome. (See neo-classic for American classical period)

Claw and ball foot A dragon or bird claw grasping a ball or pearl. Of Oriental origin. An eagle claw was most often used on American pieces. This foot was first used in the American Queen Anne period, and then more extensively in the Chippendale.

Claw foot A paw foot. A foot made to resemble a lion or dog, or eagle claw foot. Examples can be seen in the Empire and Sheraton periods. Duncan Phyfe made many pieces in the Sheraton period using the dog claw foot.

Claw table   A small table with a circular shaped top, pedestal or shaft, and tripod base with claw feet. Not to be confused with a pillar-and-claw table.

Closed arch   An arch that is not broken. Examples are on Queen Anne secretaries.

Clover leaf top   A four lobed table top taking its name from a four leaf clover. Examples found on Sheraton tables 1800 to 1810.

Club chair   A heavily upholstered chair having solid sides and a low back. Examples seen in the Empire period.

Club foot   This type of foot is found on a cabriole leg. It is also called a Dutch foot. Dutch or club feet may be in pad, trifid, slipper, or snake form. This type of foot may have a disc, shoe, or cushion under it. Club feet are most important in the Queen Anne period. A second meaning is a tapering leg with a hoof-shaped foot. Hoof feet are seen mainly on English pieces.

Cluster column legs   These are leg columns placed together in a cluster. Examples may be seen on Sheraton and Victorian pieces.

Cock beading molding   This is tiny half-circle projecting molding. Seen after 1730 on American pieces. On Sheraton pieces cock beaded was sometimes executed in brass strips.

Collar   Turning often found at base of a ball or turnip foot. Examples in William and Mary period.

Colonettes   Small columns: usually refers to "projecting colonettes" or "partial colonettes". Examples may be seen on Sheraton chests.

Colonial revival   Furniture made after 1876 adapting or copying designs of the early American periods.

Comb-back   A type of Windsor with a back resembling a comb. Comb-backs have spindles that finish upward into a comb-piece or crest-rail.

Commode A low cabinet usually enclosing shelves or deep drawers. Can be called a bureau, console, chest, or sideboard. This word usually describes English chests of drawers. Chippendale perhaps designed the first bedroom commode.

Commode chair Chair, with a deep apron, sheltering a chamber pot.

Compass decoration Circular, arc and star designs. Examples may be found incised on Puritan chests. Many Boston area desks on frame (1730-1760) inlayed a star or compass on the slant top.

Concave A hollow curve. A curve that dips inward.

Connecticut chest American chest with two rows of double drawers standing on four short legs, often decorated with split spindles that were painted black. They were called Connecticut chests because many were found in Connecticut.

Console table Table made in the form of a bracket with its back attached to the wall and its front supported by one or two legs. Examples may be seen in the Empire and Victorian periods.

Conversational An "S" shaped love seat made in the American Victorian period.

Convex A rainbow shaped curve. A "camel-hump" shaped curve.

Convolute A scroll or paper-roll shape. Examples are ears on various Chippendale chair crest rails.

Coop back A windsor with one or more geometric cage details placed between the two top back-rails. Usually bamboo turned.

Corkscrew finial Also called a flame or blaze finial. Examples of a wood corkscrew finial are seen on Newport block-front pieces on the pediment, emerging from fluted urns, in the Chippendale period.

Corner block A carved block of wood that was employed to strengthen chairs, set at the intersection of seat and legs.

Corner chair A square-seated chair with its seat placed diagonally so that one corner faces the front. A corner chair was called a roundabout. These first appeared in the Queen Anne period.

Corner cupboard   Type of cupboard which became fashionable in the 18th century. Sometimes called a china cupboard. The front was diagonal or curved. The corner cupboard was also made as a hanging cupboard.

Cornice   The horizontal molding at the top of a casepiece. William and Mary kas's had a heavy cornice. Federal casepieces had more delicate ones.

Cornucopia   A horn of plenty. Examples of this design are seen in the American Empire period painted and stenciled on stay-rails of Hitchcock chairs, often with the stay-rail cut in outline of the horn or horns. Empire sofas commonly used a cornucopia shaped leg. These usually had brass feet and casters.

Cottage furniture   Painted Victorian furniture often in Hepplewhite and Sheraton designs. Many with floral patterns. Often used in bedrooms.

Cotter-pin   Wires that are clinched on the inside (twisted) of a drawer to hold the handles and plates of a drawer pull. They were easily untwisted to allow brasses to be removed for polishing. Examples in William and Mary period.

Couch   Another name for daybed, restbed, or long chair. Examples are seen in the William and Mary period.

Country Chippendale   A mid 18th century simple form of Chippendale pieces often in pine or fruit woods. Many are simply beautiful.

Country furniture   Furniture made in small rural communities of local woods, often primitive, but employing basic designs from the urban areas. Country Chippendale pieces are a good example.

Court cupboard   A Puritan cupboard with a Jacobean heritage that had its upper portion enclosed and its lower portion open.

Court work   Ornate English pieces made for the aristocracy and Crown. America made no similar pieces.

Craft Movement   About 1882 the Arts and Craft Movement preached a revival of craftsmanship. This movement began in England.

Crescent stretcher Also called a crinoline stretcher. Examples seen on various Windsor chairs. They are attached to the front legs and supported by a short member from each back leg.

Crest-rail The top-rail of a furniture back. Crest-rails can be shaped or carved or both. William and Mary cane chairs had high-carved crest-rails. Victorian sofa crest-rails sometimes were covered with rococo designed carving, and had curved shapes.

Crinoline stretcher A semi-circular stretcher also called a crescent stretcher. Examples are seen on various Windsor chairs. They are attached to the front legs and supported by a short member from each back leg.

Cross banding A band or border where the figure of the wood runs across the width. Holly, maple, and satinwood were often used for cross-banding on Federal pieces. Massachusetts cross banded light and dark woods alternately on Sheraton pieces.

Cross-rail A horizontal bar connecting uprights of a chair-back.

Cross-stretcher "X" shaped stretcher found on occasional tables and various chairs and on particular high and lowboys. Examples appear on William and Mary pieces.

Cross-stretchered seating Chairs, stools, sofas, and settees based on Roman curule chairs. Many appear in the Sheraton period with cane backs and arms. Many have reeded legs, and paw feet on casters. The majority of sofas have cast brass lion heads at the crossing and carved back rails.

Crotch-grain Veneer generally cut from the main crotch or fork of a tree.

Cuff Inlaid bracelet. Cuffs are found on Federal pieces at the ankle on the leg. Hepplewhite tables often have cuffs. Satinwood and birch were often used.

Cup Bottom or base of a turned shaft. Examples on Chippendale tripod tea tables having a flared shaft with a cup base.

Cupboard Cabinet for food or clothing. In England it is called an "aumbry." In France it is called an "armoire."

Cup-caster   A wheel or a roller with a cup that fits over the end of a furniture leg with a privot-mounted roller beneath. They can be round or square and are usually made of brass and were used 1800 to 1840. Examples may be seen on Belter Victorian pieces.

Cupid's bow   The top-rail of a chair back having a double ogee curve resembling a bow. It is called a serpentine top-rail. These are found on Chippendale chairs. Also refers to certain Hepplewhite skirts in the same configuration.

Cup-turned   Cup shaped turning. Cup turnings are often used with trumpet turnings. Examples are seen on William and Mary legs.

Curl   A natural figure in wood that resembles a curl.

Curule chair   A neo-classical chair resembling a Roman chair with curved half-circle legs in an "X" shape. Examples may be seen on Duncan Phyfe pieces in the Sheraton period.

Curule legs   Half-circle legs in an "X" shape. These are also called Grecian Cross legs. Examples seen on various Sheraton pieces.

Cushioned pad foot   Dutch foot with a shoe or disk beneath the pad. A feature of New England pieces about 1750 to 1760.

Cut down   A piece with its legs having been shortened or "cut down".

Cylinder fall   The curved solid wood sliding top fitted to writing tables or desks. Examples may be seen in the Victorian period.

Cylinder front   A quarter round fall front of a desk that is either a solid piece or a tambour sliding up and back in quandrantal grooves. Examples may be seen on Hepplewhite desks.

Cyma curve   It is a continuous curve, half of which is concave and the other half convex. This produces a gentle "S" shape. It is pronounced si-ma. An example is the cabriole leg.

"D" shape   Refers to Federal sideboards which have a "D" shaped top and game tables with a "D" shaped top when closed.

Daybed   A long chair or chaise or lounge that was used for day rest.

Daybeds are also called "couches" or "rest beds". First seen in the William and Mary period as a chair style but a few date from the late Puritan period.

Deal Scottish or Wild Pine used for interior parts of English case-pieces. Deal was also used in England for cheap furniture in the Victorian period.

Demi-arm A partial arm seen on Victorian seating pieces. It is also called a "hip rest".

Demi-lune A half-round shape. Examples found on Federal style Hepplewhite tables.

Dentil molding Molding that resembles teeth that need braces because they have space between them.

Desk A writing surface with or without drawers or cabinets. Can be open or closed. Desks are seen from the William and Mary period. Evolved from a box on a stand.

Desk and bookcase form A bookcase having hinged door opening to shelves or partitions added to a desk unit. A secretary.

Diaper Design consisting of diamond shapes, in regular repeats, often incised carved on Puritan and Victorian pieces.

Directoire Type of French furnishings and decoration of the mid 1790's, characterized by an increasing use of Grece-Roman forms and motifs. This is referred to as a neo-classical style.

Disc foot Also called a "disk foot". A Dutch pad foot with a round shoe beneath it. The shoe is the disc. Also called a cushioned foot. Examples may be seen on Queen Anne chairs.

Dish-top A rounded table top that is dished out flat in the center leaving a rounded raised edge. Dish tops may be seen on dumbwaiters.

Disk foot A disc foot. A Dutch foot with a shoe. A cushioned foot.

Document drawer Also called a "document box". A narrow, vertical drawer that is open at the top and is placed next to the central locker in a desk interior. Document drawers are found both on American and English desks and secretaries.

Dolphin This motif appears on American Empire and American Victorian pieces as well as on English and French furniture. In the American Empire period the dolphin may appear as sofa leg supports. They were often gilded.

Doric column Can be Greek or Roman columns. The Greek do not have a base while Roman ones do. They are channeled. Doric columns have a capital at the top. These columns, usually plain and unchanneled are found on Puritan table legs and later on American Empire pieces.

Double chairs Also called "love-seats". The English call them "Darby and Joan seats". The French term is "confidantes".

Double feet A double round or double block turning. Examples may be seen on William and Mary cane chairs and bannister back chairs.

Dovetail Devices used to fasten wood together by fitting wedge-shaped or dovetail shaped pieces into corresponding negative spaces. Examples of dovetails can be seen on Chippendale casepieces. Early ones are not uniform. Dovetails are seen on ancient Egyptian furniture, proving that "if it works, don't change it".

Dowel Wood or iron pin employed for joining two pieces of wood. Dowels are used in place of screws or nails. Dowels are seen on Puritan panel chests.

Dragon's claw foot A claw and ball foot. An 18th century foot with a dragon's claw grasping a ball or pearl. These are seen on cabriole legs late in the Queen Anne period as well as in the Chippendale period. The dragon's claw foot is Oriental in origin.

Drake foot A Dutch or club foot carved with three toes, sometimes four, that somewhat resemble the contracted claw of a male duck. They are also called trifid, and web, and drake feet. A drake foot is found on cabriole legs. Examples may be seen on William and Mary pieces.

Draped torsos Draped male figures designed to support arms of certain Renaissance Revival sofas and chairs.

Drawer blades The wooden strips that separate a drawer into separate sections.

Drawer bottom Lower portion of a drawer. (Note the thickness of drawer bottoms to identify origin) English cabinetmakers used thin deal or oak while American cabinetmakers used thicker boards of poplar, pine and chestnut. The bottoms of old pieces are not smooth like later machine-finished drawer bottoms.

Draw-runner A device for supporting the drop-lid or fall-front of a desk or secretary. These are also called slides.

Drop A pendant ornament. Examples are found on William and Mary highboys.

Drop handle A pendant hardware used in a drawer pull. Examples may be seen on William and Mary tear-drop brasses.

Drop ornament This is an ornament that hangs down, usually from the underframe of a piece. Also called pendants. Examples may be seen on Queen Anne highboys.

Drop-front Also called a fall-front. The leaf falls forward and becomes the writing place. It rests on draw-runners or slides.

Drop-leaf A table with one or two hinged leaves which can be raised or dropped by bringing swinging legs or supports into position. Drop-leaf tables can be seen in the William and Mary period.

Drum table A round table. A cylindrical top table. Also called a capstan table. Usually with drawers or shelves in the skirt. Has pedestal and outcurved legs. Examples in Federal period.

Dry rot When wood shows frailty, cracking or breaking, producing a gray dry powder.

Duck foot Also called a drake, web, or trifid Dutch foot. Found on William and Mary and Queen Anne pieces.

Dumbwaiter A tiered stand made to hold serving items. An example is a three tiered Sheraton piece with graduating dished tiers, a turned pedestal column, fine base, and terminating with three outcurved legs with brass feet and castors. About 45 inches high. Circa 1815.

Duncan Phyfe (1768 - 1854) One of Americas most outstanding cabinetmakers in the Sheraton and Empire periods. His carving is legendary. He worked in New York near where the Stock Exchange is now located.

Duncan Phyfe logs Fine mahogany timbers were referred to as "Duncan Phyfe logs" because he was known for using extremely fine mahogany.

Dust-boards Large pieces of wood placed between the drawers in English casepieces to prevent stealing. American casepieces do not usually have dust-boards. However some appear in Williamsburg and Charleston casepieces.

Dutch foot A club foot found on cabriole legs. If a shoe, disc, or disk is beneath it, it is called a disc or disk foot. Varieties include a pad, trifid, (web, duck, drake) snake or slipper foot. Dutch feet can be found on American Queen Anne pieces.

Eagle This emblem, an ancient Roman symbol, has been important on American furniture. It was carved as a center finial on fine Chippendale highboys. In the Federal period as inlay and on certain chairs as splats. Hepplewhite was very partial to this design and also used it on his brasses. It appears in the Empire period and again in the Victorian.

Ears An extension of a chair's crest-rail or comb-piece beyond the back posts. When they are carved in a spiral they are called voluted. Examples are seen on Chippendale chairs with cupid's bow or serpentine back-rails. Also on various Windsor chairs.

Charles Eastlake (1836 - 1906) An influential English writer. He became identified with Gothic and Renaissance Revival furniture through many articles preaching furniture crafsmanship. Eastlake did not design any furniture but manufacturers cashed in on his popularity and called their factory machine-made furniture "Eastlake style". Eastlake was not pleased but apparently did nothing to stop his name from being used.

Easy chair   An upholstered chair. Upholstered chairs first appear in the American William and Mary period. These were the first really comfortable chairs. First use of slip covers appear with upholstered furniture in America.

Ebonized wood   Wood stained to look like real ebony. Ash and holly were frequently used for this purpose. Used for inlay in the Federal period.

Egg and dart   A convex molding with a design resembling alternating eggs and darts. Examples found on Puritan tables.

Eglomise'   Named for French 18th century artist. It is decorated glass in which the back is painted or gilded. Examples are found on Hepplewhite secretaries.

Elbow chair   A Federal upholstered back arm chair. The arms slope gently for comfort.

Elliptic front   A round front. Hepplewhite designed round-front chests of drawers.

Elliptical foot   A William and Mary circular turned foot found on various slat-back chairs with turned legs.

Empire Period   American Empire 1820-1840 (French Empire 1799-1840)

Key Words: French, architectural, columns, ormolu, stencil gilding, animal imagery, projecting top, pillar and scroll, klismos chair, lion paw foot, veneers

Empire has been the step-child of American furniture. Having a French emperor for a father was not easy for this American boy. But please, don't reject him as an overweight, overdressed kid. Duncan Phyfe called this "butcher furniture", and many historians say fine antique American furniture ends with Sheraton. Judge for yourself.

It is strong and masculine, but it is not all bulky and ponderous. It varied furniture feet with shaped bases which was a welcome change. Empire rosewood and mahogany veneers are exciting and dramatic. The seating pieces are extremely comfortable. As for the ormolu, Americans used considerably less than the French, and often substituted stencil-gilding. Military symbols indicate French pieces. Painted Hitchcock chairs are Empire pieces.

After 1814 America left the British sphere of furniture influence for the first time. The English were doing Classical Regency but Americans set our sights on French Empire. In France this furniture was called "Greek taste" or "a la Greque". We did, however, make some pieces with English Regency designs.

The French had rejected "decadent" pre-Revolutionary styles. They now desired furniture that would symbolize a new era. The style they chose evolved from the 1748 excavations at Pompeii, although classical Italians might not recognize it. This heavy furniture was enriched with porcelain plaques, marble tops, gilt, and masses of quasi-classical ormolu. These replaced earlier carved ornaments, rococo carving, and marquetry.

American Empire simplified this French style as we had simplified previous English styles. It started with a continuation of late Sheraton scale pieces and became larger and heavier at the end of the period. Americans employed curved and straight lines. Carvings disappeared and plain surfaces with architectural pillars and scrolls are late characteristics. Cabinet pieces were usually rectangular and often have beautiful white marble tops. Heavy cornices are prominent. Plain or ornamented columns appear on casepieces such as desks, secretaries and chests, recalling the columns of ancient Greece and Rome. Tall pieces such as secretaries and chests gain height in this period. The center table was a fashionable new piece, first made in New York.

Sheraton characteristics continue with saber legs that are turned, spirally reeded, or acanthus-leaf carved. Later chairs have heavy urn-shaped splats. Tables with veneered columns are circular or octagular and rest on shaped plinths and are supported by heavy scrolled, or flattened ball feet that are usually castered. Wide ogee molding faced with crotch-grain veneer was used on drawer fronts and cornices.

Empire furniture had many ormolu decorations. Some were primarily found on French pieces, such as military symbols, bees, caryadids, wreaths with a "N" inside, thunderbolts, and flying disks. Carved caryatids which depict female figures and carved Atlantes which depict male figures and are also called "mummy headed therms" and "Turk's heads" are found on legs of a group of sideboards and side tables made in Philadelphia and Baltimore. The Turk's heads are often turbaned and bearded. American pieces had griffins, winged eagles, swans, sea horses, dolphins, winged lions, pineapples, diamond patterns, wreaths, ivy, cornicopeas, and acanthus. Perhaps the most frequently used decoration is anthemia. This is Greek honeysuckle, and it appears along with acanthus motifs on many pieces.

Sofas, sideboards, and various tables, are taking on large sizes, considerable weight, and perhaps the feet of an imaginary animal. The chairs, however, are not as heavy as most Empire pieces. This characteristic continues into the Victorian period.

The arms of Empire chairs began high on the uprights of the back, curved down and ended in a scroll. The backs were low and the top or crest rail was often curved or looped. The wide splat was urn shaped and was veneered. The seat is a slip seat with a bowed or curved front. The seat rail follows this curve. Certain chairs had cane seats. The front legs are turned forward and the back legs curve backwards following the line of the chair back. This chair was also made with a horizontal splat. Casters are seen on the front legs. These chairs were inspired by the ancient Greek klismos chair. Rockers were made in this style.

There were also simple upholstered chairs that had a Restoration background. These were square and simple with straight backs and straight legs. They resemble a contemporary club chair and are extremely comfortable. Another Empire arm-chair was upholstered and had a high curved back framed by uprights with the "Empire" backward curve. The top-rail is concave. This is an open-arm chair with upholstered arm pads. The arms end in a "C" scroll. The rear legs curve backwards and the front ones have bold turnings

75

or are made in a reverse curve. Casters were put on all four legs of this chair. Rockers were also made in this style.

French Empire chairs with arms resting on griffins, swans, or lions are called "throne chairs". These have front legs that are turned and gilded, and back ones that curve backwards. Various arm chairs were made showing English Regency influences. John Hewitt from New York was known for producing especially beautiful arm chairs.

Sofas have a straight or shaped top rail, with the ends curving down. Those with a straight top may have a single panel outlined with molding and the top ends concavely. Almost all the sofas evoke "roll-over arms". Fine Sheraton curves get lost when sofas assume a variety of heavy shapes late in this period.

Carving is seen on Empire sofas and they usually were supported by four brackets with casters, or by animal legs with carved knees. Legs were carved wings ending in paws or, eagle heads, or dolphins, or they had large round turnings called melon turnings. The legs also became plain heavy scrolls. The backs of Empire sofas were 31 to 35 inches high and the length was 6 feet 6 inches to 8 feet.

The Empire period also made a romantic Grecian couch. This had a high headrest at one end. It was called a "Recamier" sofa. It was supported by cornucopia brackets ending with brass paw feet of animal leg brackets terminating in carved paw feet or large down curved scrolled brackets or rectangular plinths above block feet. They are 34 to 40 inches high and 6 to 7-1/2 feet long.

The American Empire style also produced a slant or fall-front desk similar to what was seen in the Queen Anne period. What is different are the columns at the sides and the large turned feet or the carved paw feet. These desks were made in a variety of woods including mahogany, with crotch-grain veneer, cherry, maple, and birch. Some have ormolu mounts.

Secretaries were also produced in the Empire style. These pieces showed the Sheraton influence, but did not use pull brackets to support the writing flap, but supported the writ-

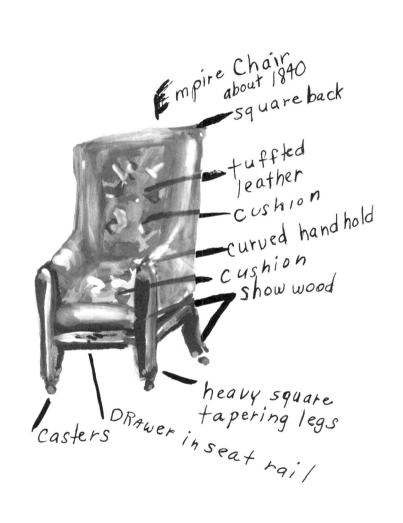

Empire Chair
about 1840
square back

tuffted
leather
cushion

curved hand hold
cushion
show wood

heavy square
tapering legs

Casters

DRAwer in seat rail

Oval
escutcheons

brass
surrounds

rosettes of
stamped brass
with
cast
ring
handles

A circular plate is
also seen (early)

Lion's head
stamped brass
with
cast
ring
handle

Empire Mounts
include brass rosette
knobs and pressed glass knobs

Handles of
mushroom shaped
wood

ing part with the top drawer. They have columns like the ones seen on the chests. The pilasters are carved or reeded. The feet are turned or paw carved. The top or upper section of the secretaries have a flat cornice, some of which overhang. Beneath were bookshelves with glass doors that were often designed with Gothic arches. These doors had wood glazing bars in designs that were usually geometric. On these pieces we find wooden knobs or pressed glass knobs. These pieces were eight or nine feet tall.

Desks with cylinder closings and gallery tops relating to the Louis XVI bureau (a' cylindre) were made in America between 1815 to 1825. These had curved sides and reeded legs with brass feet.

The sideboards show the characteristics found on other Empire pieces. The top overhangs the casepiece. There are usually two wide cupboards with a tier of full or half-width drawers. The sideboards are out to six feet long with plain or reeded columns and turned or carved paw feet. Some sideboards have a tambour front section and galleries.

There were two principal types of dining tables produced in the period. One was the drop-leaf, with four, plain, spirally reeded or carved legs that had brass casters. The other was the pedestal base drop-leaf table. The pedestal column is circular or rectangular and has four carved legs that have carved paw or flattened ball feet or a concave scroll instead of feet.

The early Empire card table has a rounded skirt. The later ones are straight. The top folds over and they are usually on a pedestal base or with four legs similar to the ones seen on dining tables.

A table with the Empire interpretation of the Sheraton "pillar and claw" table with a massive center column, four incurved legs and brass paw feet was often used for card playing and was called a "loo table".

The work or sewing tables are 22 to 26 inches wide with plain skirts, usually two drawers, and with regular Empire legs or pedestal. Some are stenciled. The sleigh bed, Grecian couch, Boston rocker and the Hitchcock chair are new pieces.

The Hitchcock chair was first produced in Connecticut and was sold for use in meeting places, as was the earlier Windsor chair from the Queen Anne period. Lambert Hitchcock who created this chair, began to mass produce them at a factory level. Eventually "Hitchcock" became the name for a variety of painted and stenciled chairs. These chairs, although of the Empire period, did not have the "Empire" look but resemble Sheraton pieces instead. The multiple ring turned legs that tapered to a small ball were a prominent feature of these chairs. The stay-rail was stenciled. Another feature was the turned pillow-back top rail. The seats were rush or cane.

The Empire bedroom dressers have prominent tops with tiers of drawers. Wide ogee molding faced with crotch-grain veneer was used for drawer fronts. On many chests, the top drawer overhangs the lower drawers and this overhang is supported by columns. Some columns are plain. Others ornamented with ring turning, reeding, or carving, and some with quilted pineapple designs. Some of the dressers have half round columns which are decorated with heavy carving. Columns that are ornamented at both top and bottom with a cylinderical and carved design were designated as "pineapples". This design is also seen on beds. These dressers were about 14 inches higher than those in the Hepplewhite or Sheraton period.

(Mounts) The brasses on Empire furniture are stamped brass rosettes, with acanthus leaves and with a ring hanging from a post in the middle, and a cast brass lion's head (mask) with a circle between its jaws. Sideboards with animal feet generally have brass lion head mounts. The escutcheons are stamped ovals or inset keyhole surrounds. Round stamped brass knobs with patriotic designs are seen on early pieces. Other handles are round mushroom turned knobs made of wood. Pressed glass mushroom shaped knobs in blue, green, and yellow, are seen in opaque or clear glass. Some of these handles resemble pressed glass plate patterns.

Most French Empire pieces were made of mahogany, ebony, rosewood, burr elm, burr ash, satinwood and fruitwood. Marble is important on French pieces. Handles were cast lion's masks with a ring or in gilt bronze knobs.

English Regency cabinetmakers were considerably influenced by French taste under Napoleon. They applied ormolu to surfaces where the French would never dream of doing so. Some of these pieces are curiosities.

(Important Empire cabinetmakers) Noted furniture makers in the American Empire period were Charles-Honore' Lannuier, the workshop of Duncan Phyfe, and workshop of Williams and Dawson, Anthony Querville, John Needles, John Finlay, Thomas Hope, George Smith and Rudolph Ackerman.

(Woods) Mahogany with crotch-grain is the featured wood in the American Empire period. It has marvelous color tones that range from yellowish or pinkish tones to deep reddish or purplish-brown hues. Mahogany has beautiful pattern figures. Santo Domingo mahogany had little figures, while Cuban mahogany was primarily cut for veneers. Fiddle-back figures are found primarily on Honduras mahogany. The timber from Jamaica is dark and rich toned. The "plum-pudding" — "plum-mottle" mahogany looks like dark elliptical marks. "Roe" is a term given to dark flakes in a figure which give an effect of dark and light not unlike certain effects in Rembrandt's paintings called "chiroscuro". As stated in the other periods, mahogany possesses a capacity for repelling larvae that damage other furniture. Mahogany does not gray from exposure to sunlight.

Rosewood furniture was made in the late Empire period. Rosewood is a hard wood. Rosewood from Brazil ranges in color from yellowish-tan through orange and deeper red tones to a very dark purplish color. Rosewood also came from Madagascar. This medium rose-pink wood had prominent veinings in a deeper reddish tone. This wood has brownish-black or black figure pigments and can have ivory colored streaks. The name comes from the fact that when it is sawed, a scent of roses is observed.

American black cherry grows throughout the eastern half of America, except in Florida. Cherry is a light reddish-tan. The timber is hard and has a straight grain with small pores. In some cuttings, a mild type of ring growth figure is seen and in rare instances swirl, feather, crotch or wavy figures are found.

Maple was also used in the American Empire period. Mostly the rock or sugar maple, which grew throughout the eastern half of America. Maple can be a light-creamy-tan to a deeper pinkish tan. It is a hard, strong wood, and has a fine texture. Maple has very interesting grain figures described as fiddle-back, curly, tiger-stripe, and bird's eye markings. Curly maple was important in the Empire period and was used on casepieces and for bedroom furniture.

Empire bed   Another name for a "Napoleon" bed or "sleigh" bed having a backrolled foot and head.

Escallop   An English term. Also called scallop or shell. A flat shell with curved scallops. This motif was often seen in the Queen Anne period. The Dutch call it a cockle shell. The English a scallop or escallop. In America "shell" or "fan" is used.

Escutcheon   A shield-shaped piece that covers the keyhole. Escutcheons are first seen on American pieces in the William and Mary period. Can be metal, ivory or wood.

Etagere   A series of open shelves. Many examples appear in the Victorian period. Some were made to stand in corners. "What not" is also an American description.

Extension table   A table which opens from the center and moves in both directions in order to make room for loose leaves in the open part. Examples are seen on Sheraton period dining tables. Contemporary tables are often constructed this way.

Faceted table tops   A rare Philadelphia design from 1730 to 1760. They simplified seating by indicating chair placement by angle. Examples appear with up to twelve-sided tops or drop-leaf tables, with cabriole legs, some with stockings on their pad feet. These were very expensive pieces.

Fake   A copy of an authentic piece made to be sold as if it were "the real thing". A fake is a piece made with intent to deceive.

Fall front   A desk board which hinges from an upright position to a flat writing surface. Also called a drop-front or slope-front. Examples can be seen on Queen Anne and Chippendale desks.

Fan   Carved shell motif came in England from a Dutch cockleshell design. We first see it in our Queen Anne period. This stylized shell with fluted rays in a half-circle (half-round) has many names. It can be called a shell, a fan, a rising sun, and a sunrise. In England it is called a sunburst. Benjamin Franklin in a discussion with James Madison said it was definitely a sunrise and not a sunset. Madison accepted his opinion and I would not contradict Franklin. A full fan (a full circle) can be called a "pinwheel" or a "full sunrise". The English prefer a "full sunburst". This detail was employed often in the Queen Anne period. Examples are also found on Chippendale block and shell pieces, and inlayed on many Federal pieces.

Fancy chair   An occasional chair, usually of light weight, often with a cane, rush, or painted seat, and painted body. Painted chairs were important in England in our Hepplewhite period. In America they are seen in the Sheraton period. These pieces can be simple or highly decorated and gilded. Many are absolutely beautiful. They were often made in sets for dining rooms.

Federal style   In America "Federal" describes furniture made between 1783-1820s. It includes Hepplewhite, Sheraton, and early Empire.

Festoons   Strings or chains carved, inlaid, or painted to resemble ribbons, draperies, or foliage or flowers. Examples are seen on Sheraton furniture.

Fiddle-back   A single splat of a chair which has a fiddle shape. Narrow fiddle shapes are also called "spoon shaped". Examples are seen on Queen Anne chairs.

Fiddle-string or stick-back   Terms referring to the backs of Windsor chairs with the spindles resembling sticks or fiddle strings.

Fielded panels   Raised panels. Examples on various Chippendale casepieces.

Figures   Timber designs, brought out by cutting the wood so that veneers or solid surfaces display various types of irregularities in the grain and in color. Fiddle-back figures are found primarily in Honduras mahogany. Black cherry has a mild ring growth figure. Sugar maple has tiger-stripe figures.

Finger-grip   A groove indented in the lower edge of a drawer-front or on a wooden handle. These can be seen in the Victorian period.

Finger-roll   Continuous concave molding in the frame of a piece. Examples can be seen on Victorian sofa frames and chair frames.

Finial   A decorative ornament that points upward. Examples in acorn, knob and double knob designs can be seen on Puritan chairs, and on Chippendale casepieces such as highboys and secretaries as blazes and eagles. They are also found on many Federal casepieces as gilded balls, brass balls, eagles, urns and cone-shaped pinetrees. Finials are also found on table stretchers in the Victorian period.

Fish-tail pendant   A rare detail found on highboy and lowboy skirts between pairs of diminutive semi-circles. This is a Philadelphia or Pennsylvania trait seen on casepieces from about 1735-1760.

Fittings   The metal handles or escutcheons on furniture. Also called mounts.

Flame   A finial carved in a spiral or flame shape. These finials are also called a blaze or corkscrew.

Flat carving   Also called peasant carving, relief carving or incised carving. Flat carving is seen on Puritan pieces and later in the Victorian period on Renaissance Revival pieces.

Flemish curve   "S" scroll used in the William and Mary period and in preceding periods. This curve can be seen on William and Mary cane chairs on the crest-rail, legs and stretchers.

Flip-top table   A card or game table with a hinged top, made in two parts. Many examples can be seen on Federal pieces.

Flutes   An inlay design resembling the musical instrument. Sometimes the central flute dips below the two side ones. On Townsend Newport pieces the central flute is always higher.

This design is also seen on various Federal card tables on the apron above center legs.

Fluting A series of rounded convex furrows or channels cut vertically on a column, leg, shaft, pilaster, or canted edge. The opposite of "reeding" which is raised. Many Chippendale pieces have fluting on their canted corners.

Fly rail The swinging bracket which supports a flap or drop leaf.

Flying chairs Light weight Victorian chairs made after 1851. They were made to move freely around the room. They were constructed of a light wood from Africa.

Flying disks Decorative flat disks centered between two outspread wings. Also called winged orbs. Egyptian in origin and seen on American Empire pieces as well as on French Empire pieces. Also on Victorian furniture with Egyptian designs.

Flying leg A leg on Federal card tables that moved to support the top when open.

Folding stand A tip-table. These were made throughout the colonies in tripod form, some with the bird cage detail.

Frame The basic skeleton of a piece of furniture.

French cabinets Large cabinets appearing around 1860 in the American Victorian period. They were ornately carved with medallions and cabochons, with marquetry, having heavy finials on the back portion, with marble tops, gilt, cherubs, brass and painted ornamentation, enamel plaques, and Ionic capitals. Many were of ebonized wood. (Some people can't believe these cabinets are American)

French chair The name Chippendale gave to his upholstered sidechairs.

French foot A slightly out-turned rather tall bracket foot that is always combined with an apron or skirt. They are about 8 to 10 inches tall. They can be seen on many Hepplewhite chests of drawers. Shaker casepieces with French type feet, without an apron or skirt, are the only exception.

French polished Highly shellacked. French polishing gives furniture a glass-like finish. It also may cause the surface of a piece to become cloudy or produce reddish streaks.

French whorl foot A foot which is swirled or curled inwards. Seen on various Chippendale pieces and also on Victorian furniture having a French rococo flavor.

Frieze A decorative band. Examples are seen on American and English tall chests at the top under the cornice.

Fret-work Ornamental work consisting of three dimensional designs within a band or border. They are an applied decoration. Examples are found on Chinese Chippendale pieces.

Fruitwood Used mainly for country furniture with the exception of cherry.

Gadroon edges A decoration resembling almond shaped reeding or fluting. Gadrooned edges were very fashionable in New York and Philadelphia during the Chippendale period. Heavy gadrooning is associated with New York pieces.

Gallery An ornamental rail or cresting in wood or metal surrounding the top of a table, desk, or stand. Examples may be found scalloped in wood on various Hepplewhite tables.

Games tables Also called card tables. These were small tables popular in the 18th century. Various ones had reversible tops with an inlaid chess board on one side. This top slid out so the backgammon board beneath could be used. Some had guinea pockets for chips and out-rounded or out-squared corners for candlesticks. Some had "let-in" tops.

Garters Seen carved, applied and inlaid on English cabriole legs below the knee. Not an American design. We have stockings and bracelets but not garters.

Gate-leg-table Also called a flap-table. A table with fall-leaves supported by folding legs that resemble a gate. Gate-leg-tables were popular in the Puritan period.

Gentlemans secretary A Sheraton piece. A cabinet combined with a writing table, having square tapering legs. Usually with banding and inlaid ovals as decoration. This piece is a wider version of his lady's secretary.

Gesso A plaster and glue preparation for underpainting or gilding. On English japanned pieces gesso was thickly applied under the ground color to give dimension to the chinoiserie designs.

Gilded ball finial   Round onion shaped piece, gilded, with a spear-like projection. A decoration found on cornices and bonnets of tall pieces like secretaries. Examples on many Federal pieces like secretaries.

Gilding   A thin layer of gold applied to furniture. Singular gilded pieces were produced in Philadelphia. Entire gilded pieces are usually associated with English and French furniture. The William and Mary period gilded their japanned pieces. The Chippendale period saw the gilding of shells on highly decorated pieces and on some fluted columns. Sheraton fancy chairs often had stencil gilding. The Empire period often substituted gilding for ormolu. Gilding appears on particular pieces in the Victorian period. Examples are Egyptian style furniture and paper mache pieces.

Glazed   Fitted or set with glass. Federal secretaries had glazed doors in their upper sections.

Glazing bars   Wood strips which frame the glass panes. Also known as muntins. Examples on Federal and Empire secretaries.

John Goddard   (1724-1785) An American furniture designer and maker from Rhode Island. He is famous for Chippendale block-and-shell pieces. These might be the most important pieces of furniture ever made in America.

Gondole chair   An Empire chair taking its shape from a Venetian gondola whose back curves forward at both sides to form the arms. Usually upholstered it is high-backed. Various Empire chairs, not upholstered have a gondole shaped top-rail.

Goose neck   A broken arch pediment. Called a swan neck when the curve is nearly vertical. Seen on Chippendale tall pieces.

Gothic   The Gothic period was 1150 to 1500. It featured pointed or lancet arches.

Gothic revival period   Early 19th century in England and America. Gothic revival was an influence in the American Victorian period. It was more important in the English Victorian period than in the American period. Our Victorian period made gothic revival pieces primarily as hall and library furniture.

Gouge carving   A type of carving with the designs gouged out with chisels. Examples of gouge carving are seen on certain frame chests in the Puritan period.

Grain painting   Technique of applying paint to imitate the grain of wood. Grain painting has a long English history. This was first done in America in the Puritan period. It was very fashionable in the 19th century, especially in rural regions where imported wood was very expensive.

Great chairs   Carved Puritan wainscot chairs reserved for important persons.

Grecian couch   A late 19th century lounge with one arm higher than the other. Also called a Recamier sofa. It was an American and French Empire period piece. This piece is basically a daybed.

Grecian cross-legs   Another name for curule legs. These are seen on Sheraton pieces and again in the Victorian period.

Grotesque   Describes fantasy in the shaping of forms carved on furniture. An example is on highly decorated wainscot chairs from Massachusetts in the Puritan period.

Guinea pockets   Four shallow saucers found on card table tops for chips or money. Also called scoops and money dishes. These are seen on Chippendale game tables. The English referred to them as "guinea holes". The Country term is fish ponds.

"H" stretcher   A stretcher in a "H" shape. Examples may be seen on Chinese Chippendale chairs.

Half-column   A split column set against a flat surface. These may also be called a rounded pilaster. Examples are seen on Chippendale casepieces.

Handhold   The end of a chair arm where the hand rests.

Handles   See mounts.

Handkerchief table   Tables with a closed triangular top that forms a square "handerchief" when open. Examples in Queen Anne period.

George Hepplewhite   An English designer. 1785-1800. A major

American period is named for him. This is the period immediately after the Revolutionary War. Hepplewhite is famous for his shield-back chairs.

Hepplewhite period   Hepplewhite period 1785-1800 (English 1770-1790)

Key Words: Federal, delicate, slender, inlay, spade foot, French foot, shield-back, urn, eagle, tapering leg

The Chippendale period ended with the Revolutionary War and the Hepplewhite period began about 1785. It incorporated the designs of the Adam brothers and was greatly influenced by discoveries at Pompeii in Italy. This period is "Federal" in style and Neo-Classical in design. Neo-Classism describes the style recycling antique Greek, Etruscan, Roman, and Egyptian motifs.

George Hepplewhite, another Georgian English cabinetmaker and designer was a contemporary of Thomas Chippendale. Hepplewhite, as a period, came after Chippendale because Hepplewhite designs became popular at a later time. Hepplewhite's "The Cabinetmaker and Upholsterer's Guide" was published by his wife after his death in 1788. This is the first period where an English design book instead of English examples was relied upon. Hepplewhite designs were more technically accurate than Chippendale's designs.

Hepplewhite brought back the elegant simplicity of Queen Anne but in a lighter form. His pieces are delicate and graceful. Instead of the curved cabriole leg the Hepplewhite leg is slender, square and tapering. The ball and claw foot is no longer used. The spade foot on these square tapering legs is characteristic of Hepplewhite as is the French foot with connecting valanced skirts. Simple satinwood inlay is the prime decoration on fine mahogany veneered pieces that have spring bellflowers and icicles raining down their tapered legs. Urns, oval patera, lunettes and eagles were also inlaid. Maple and birch were also used for inlay.

The legs of chairs are fluted or molded. These legs and front rails could be inlaid with satinwood, birch or maple. Certain tapered legs had inlaid cuffs. Some side-chairs have incurving back legs. Salem and Philadelphia furniture makers followed Hepplewhite's patterns and incurved the rear legs but not all craftsmen followed this detail. The spade foot is the Hepplewhite trademark, although it will continue into the Sheraton period. Various chairs have square front legs, canted back legs, and a stretcher. These are early in the period and still exhibit the Chippendale influence.

Hepplewhite was most famous for his shield-back chairs. These chairs have distinctive backs that are shield-shaped, shaped with entwined hearts, intertwined ovals, lyre designs, ovals with openwork, splats, or bannisters. The splats may be designed wheat-ears, leaves, or the famous plumes called "Prince of Wales feathers". The Prince of Wales was a patron of Hepplewhite and these were designed in his honor. The same could not be said of the Queen.

The backs of Hepplewhite chairs were supported by a rail above the seat which joined the curved continuations of the back legs. The arms, if the chair has arms, are open and bowed and are supported by curved arm-stumps that are set behind the front legs. Hepplewhite arms are less curved and sometimes shorter than the later Sheraton arms on open-arm chairs.

Hepplewhite seats are outflared and frequently rounded at the back. They are rectangular in shape and the fronts can be straight or serpentine. They are slip-seats or upholstered seats that cover the seat-rail. The upholstered type were often finished with large brass tacks that were applied straight or in patterns.

English Hepplewhite painted chairs were decorated with painted ribbons and flowers. Painted chairs became important in America in the Sheraton period which followed. They were called "fancy chairs" and will be described in the Sheraton period. Some English Hepplewhite chairs were made entirely of satinwood. This is not an American trait.

Wing chairs continued to be made in the Hepplewhite period.

The wing chairs look similar to Chippendale chairs except for the legs. Chippendale used the cabriole leg with a claw and ball foot. Hepplewhite wing chairs have straight legs tapering on the inside towards the bottom and spade feet are a detail often found. Occasionally stretchers are seen on these chairs. The wing chairs have their upholstery brought down completely over the frame. The upholstered wings and arms are thinner than those on the Chippendale chair. The backs continue to display a round or serpentine shape, and there are variations in the curved backs.

Hepplewhite called his "Martha Washington" type chair a "lolling chair". It was high-backed and open-armed. The seat was lightly flared and the upholstery covered the seat rail. The legs are square and tapered and the back legs are canted. They are braced with a "H" or box stretchers. The English counterpart to this chair is called a "Gainsborough" chair. It was named for the English portrait painter who painted many of his subjects in this type of chair. (If you are in New York, you could stop in at Israel Sack and comment on a beautiful "Martha Washington" chair, and stop one floor down at Malcom Franklin and see a beautiful "Gainsborough chair").

Double chairs or loveseats continue to be made in this period. Hepplewhite referred to his upholstered chairs as "cabriole chairs".

Hepplewhite style sofas date from 1785 to 1800. Two forms were made. The earliest follows the Chippendale influence with roll-over arms and a serpentine back. The later ones are very different and are more representative of Hepplewhite. The back has a different curve with the top-rail arched and terminating in downward curves. The top-rail is not covered with upholstery. The visible top-rail continues down to form unupholstered arms and then connects with the front legs. The back is 29 to 31 inches high. The eight legs on these sofas are slender and tapered and sometimes are inlaid. The front legs may end with spade feet. The rear or back ones are square and canted. All eight were frequently castered. The legs may have lightly carved or inlaid decorations as well as the top-rail. Motifs include inlaid bellflowers, acanthus leaves, medallions, and sprays of husks.

Long couches with narrow upholstered seats were made. These often have reeded supports and arms. These are considered Hepplewhite innovations. Sheraton will use this design in the period that follows.

"Bar-Back" is Hepplewhite's own term for a curved chair-back setee. American craftsmen used Hepplewhite's designs for this piece but simplified it. American furniture craftsmen thus converted designs from a book and made them into beautiful pieces such as this setee.

The Hepplewhite period introduced the new dining room sideboard. Sideboards are side tables with added storage cabinets. Sideboards were immediately welcomed because one piece took the place of three. They were made all along the Atlantic coast where Hepplewhite furniture was very important. The front was designed with a serpentine curve. For identification purposes it must be emphasized that if the ends of the curve are concave it is a Hepplewhite sideboard. If the serpentine curve is convex it is a Sheraton sideboard. These Hepplewhite pieces are slender and delicate. The English counterparts are larger. The six legs are square and tapered with some having the new spade foot as an added detail. The interior legs are sometimes set in diagonally. These sideboards are inlaid in an elegant fashion, and finished with veneered and beaded drawers. The drawers often have fan inlays at the corners. The serpentine front sideboard is five to seven feet long. They are 40 to 44 inches high. Hepplewhite sideboards are also designed in bow, half-moon, and straight fronts. The serpentine front is seen most often.

Hepplewhite also made a break-front sideboard with a writing compartment with a fall front drawer that pulls half way out and has quadrant brackets made of brass. Most Hepplewhite sideboards are faced with mahogany using satinwood or curly maple or birch for panels and banding made of satinwood, birch, holly and stained ash for contrast. They were also made in cherry with curly maple or bird's-eye maple veneered panels.

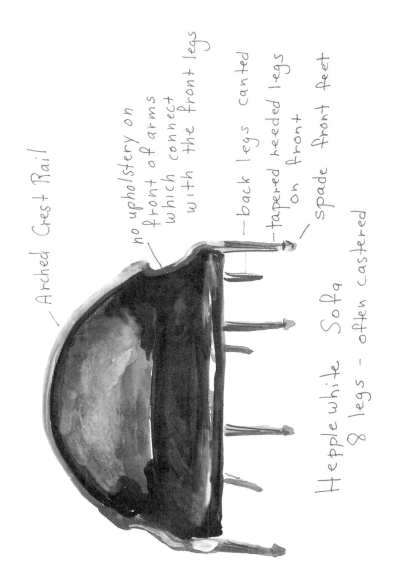

— Arched Crest Rail

no upholstery on
front of arms
which connect
with the front legs

— back legs canted

— tapered reeded legs
on front

spade front feet

Hepplewhite Sofa
8 legs - often castered

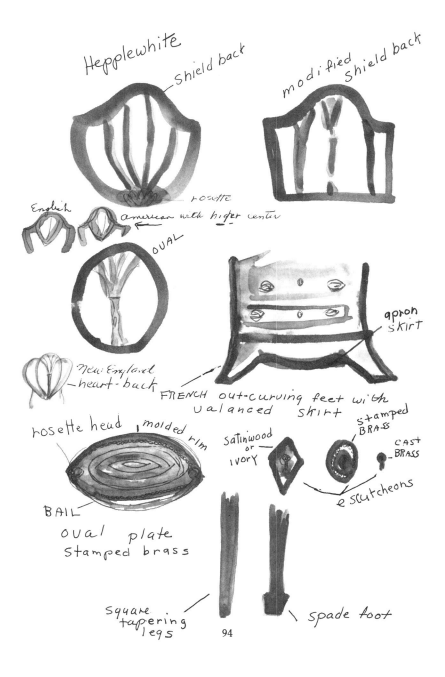

Hepplewhite

Shield back

modified Shield back

rosette

English   american with higer center

OVAL

New England
heart-back

apron
skirt

FRENCH out-curving feet with
valanced   skirt

rosette head   molded rim

satinwood
or
ivory

stamped
BRASS

CAST
BRASS

escutcheons

BAIL

oval plate
stamped brass

square
tapering
legs

spade foot

The standard New York sideboard was longer and deeper (about 6 feet long and 21 inches deep) than a sideboard made in Philadelphia (generally 5 feet long and 15 inches deep). In Maryland sideboard tables without drawers or sideboards with one row of drawers under the top were called "hunt tables".

Hepplewhite introduced the tambour feature on some desks and secretary bookcases. The term "tambour" refers to a series of small strips of wood glued on a piece of canvas or strong cloth in a manner as to produce a flexible sheet. The cabinetmakers of the Federal period used the tambour lid in preference to other lids because it was flexible, took less space, and can simply slide to either side. Hepplewhite tambours are always vertical. Also tambours contributed to the lightness of the piece, the fall front lids being heavy. The tambour secretary bookcases have glass paneled doors set in wood glazing bar moldings, often in diamond patterns, many with three panels, and often with a gothic arch at the top. Finials or urns are frequently found on the top of these pieces which are veneered and inlaid with stringing and ovals and often have husks or festoons worked into the piece. These pieces did not have secret compartments like the slant-top desks in the preceding periods. The legs of these pieces have tapered legs. Eglomise decoration is found on some secretaries.

Most break-front secretaries will come later in the Sheraton period but will expand from under six feet to eight feet in height. Secretaries often had glazed doors with geometric shaped glass in glazing bars.

Hepplewhite also made slant-front desks that had French splayed feet with a curved apron. These pieces were often inlaid. Medallions were often placed in the center of the fall-front and on the upper drawers. The major difference from the Chippendale desks is that the feet are no longer ball and claw and that they are decorated with inlay.

Hepplewhite chests are characterized by fine inlay work. They have tall bracket feet that curve a little outwards. This foot is called a French bracket foot. The skirt or apron may be scalloped and curves down at the center. Hepplewhite often gave his chests a "swell front". The straight front chest was also made.

Hepplewhite craftsmen made tripod candle stands with tops that were square, oblong, or eight-sided with simple legs, many with snake or spade feet. While Chippendale tripod feet turn up, Hepplewhite has tapered ones. Some tripod tables have spade feet as well.

Hepplewhite card tables were often made in pairs and also used for pier tables. They do not have the guinea pockets that the Chippendale tables had. They have a two leaf fold-over top. They can be circular or square and are inlaid like other Hepplewhite pieces. On rare occasions a shallow drawer is seen. They have four tapering legs. The right back one swings on a bracket to support the fold-over leaf when the table is open.

Work tables with sewing bags hanging down were also made in this period.

Another new piece was the large dining table which was constructed in two, three, and even four parts. These consisted of two half-round tables, and one or two central tables with wide leaves supported by swinging legs. Some seated twenty-four people. Pencil line inlays and stylized flowers adorned these pieces. The legs are tapered.

Highboys and lowboys were not popular in this period. Hepplewhite saw an increased use of occasional pieces such as tea tables and bookcases. Half-round card tables were also popular.

(Mounts)   About 1780 a new type of drawer handle was introduced. This was a bail-pull attached to an oval brass plate. These were stamped or embossed with designs of spread eagles with thirteen stars, a sheaf of wheat, a horn of plenty, acorns, grapes, oak leaves or similar designs. Three kinds of keyhole escutcheons are found on Hepplewhite pieces. One is a vertical oval with a beaded rim; the second is a cast brass keyhole surround; and the third is a diamond shaped inlay of satinwood veneer or ivory.

These oval mounts will be found on casepieces with French feet and tables or secretaries or desks with tapering legs.

(Important Hepplewhite cabinetmakers)   Some important furniture makers in the Hepplewhite period were Samuel McIntire, Matthew Egerton, Sr., John Townsend, Holmes Weaver, Sticker and Clemmens, John and Thomas Seymour and John Shaw.

(Woods)   The Hepplewhite period used hard, close-grained woods. Mahogany and cherry often paired with satinwood or bird's-eye maple were favored.

Mahogany is a wonderful cabinet wood. Because of the large diameter of old mahogany trees, table leaves made of this wood are practically always of one piece. Mahogany is a tropical wood of great strength and firm texture with a variety of grains and figures. The boards could be 12 feet wide. The color range is from a deep reddish-brown to yellowish or pinkish tones. Mahogany does not shrink appreciably and warps less than any other wood. It polishes beautifully. This fine wood came from Honduras and the West Indian Islands, Jamaica, Puerto Rico, Cuba and Santo Domingo. The heartwood that mahogany possesses has a capacity for repelling larvae that damage furniture woods. Marked timbers display stripe curls and mottle effects and blister, and fiddleback and plum-pudding figures. Full crotch figures were featured in the Hepplewhite period. With the Hepplewhite and later Sheraton and Empire periods, flashy figures in veneers came into vogue.

East Indian satinwood belongs to the mahogany family and is obtained principally from Ceylon. It varies from light to dark golden tones and has a fine uniform texture. The grain is narrowly interlocked. It is hard, compact and brittle, is remarkably lustrous, and takes a fine polish. It is generally unsuited to large scale furniture. It is used in general for cross bandings. In England satinwood was used for entire pieces.

American black cherry or wild cherry grows throughout the

eastern half of America, except in southern Florida. Cherry is a light reddish tan. The wood is hard, and has a straight grain with small pores. In some cuttings a mild type of ring growth figure is seen and in rare instances, swirl, feather-crotch or wavy figures is found. Cherry is heavier than maple.

Bird's-eye maple was used with other woods in the Hepplewhite period. Pieces that were made entirely of this wood belong predominately to later factory made pieces. The color tones vary from a light brownish yellow to rich amber. The bird's-eye markings are a darker tone and resemble bird's eyes. Rock or sugar maple grow throughout the eastern half of the United States and in lower Canada.

Birch is hard and close fibered and has more grain pattern than maple. It takes a high polish and when finished is light brown to yellow-amber in color. Birch often replaced expensive satinwood for stringing during the Hepplewhite period.

Herter Brothers, Gustave-Christian   New York furniture makers. Excelled in Louis XVI style.

Hickory wood   A tough wood that was used mostly for seats. It was difficult to work or nail because of hardness.

High chest   A high or tall chest of drawers, starting above the feet. Many were made in the Chippendale period.

Highboy   A chest of drawers that is on a frame or on a low boy. The lower part has one long drawer or two smaller ones. The word "highboy" is uniquely American. In England the word "tallboy" is used. These pieces were first made in the William and Mary period in America.

Hitchcock chair   Named for Lampert Hitchcock of Connecticut. An American Empire painted chair that is an American adaptation of the Sheraton painted and stenciled chair. It was sold for use in meeting places as was the earlier Windsor chair. It had multiple ring-turned legs that tapered to a small ball. It had an oval-turned pillow-back top-rail. It was usually painted black with stencillings of fruit and flowers in stencil gilding and color. The seats were rush or cane. These chairs were made from 1820 to 1850.

Hocked legs   Cabriole legs in England were and are often referred to as "hock or hocked" legs.

Holly   A hard white wood with a slightly flecked grain that was used for inlay and stringing. Dyed black it was used as a substitute for ebony. Much of the holly used on American pieces came from New Jersey.

Hoop back   Type of back design which usually identifies a Queen Anne chair with a curved crest-rail that is also called a yoke-back, but can also refer to a Windsor chair whose back forms a continuous curve or hoop.

Hunzinger   Victorian furniture maker. Worked in Louis style.

Hunt table   A sideboard table without drawers. Examples in Hepplewhite period. Also called a Hunt Board.

Husk   A motif resembling a husk of wheat. It was often used on American Federal style furniture. Sometimes husks were arranged in swags.

Icicles   Geometric inlays shaped like an icicle. Examples found on Hepplewhite legs.

Incised carving   Shallow carving. Also called intagilo carving. Examples are found on Puritan chests. Other examples are found combined with relief carving on Newport Chippendale pieces. Incised carving was done in the Empire and also in the Victorian period.

Inlay   Inserting wood of a contrasting color or texture into the surface of a piece for decoration. When inlay is done in straight lines it is called stringing. Inlay was used extensively in the Hepplewhite and Sheraton periods. Brass is also an inlay material.

Inset corner   More detailed than a simple notched corner. This corner traces the table top's molded shape. The effect is a contoured pleat. Examples on front corners of Queen Anne dressing tables. Circa 1760.

Intaglio carving   Incised designs. Examples on Chippendale casepieces and on Newport high chests on shell bases. Appears again in Victorian period.

Intermediate legs   Turned folding legs found on Sheraton dining tables, that could be folded down to support a pedestal table when leaves were added. When the leaves were removed the intermediate legs folded up. Examples seen on various Duncan Phyfe dining tables.

Invected corner   A pinched or indented corner. Examples seen on Queen Anne lowboys.

Japanning   Lacquering of pieces in the Oriental style. In America This practice began in the William and Mary period. Our finest japanned pieces were made in Boston, Philadelphia and New York. Hitchcock chairs of the early 1800's were often sold as japanned pieces. More under William and Mary period.

Kas   A large wardrobe with bun feet made in the William and Mary period. Pennsylvania Germans who also made a similar piece referred to it as a "skonk".

Kite back   A diamond splat seen on some New York Chippendale chairs.

Klismos   A classic Greek type chair with a concave back-rail and curved legs. Duncan Phyfe used this style in the Sheraton period. It was also popular in the Empire and Victorian period.

Knee   The outcurved portion of a cabriole leg. It is also called a "hip".

Knob foot   A small round turned foot. Examples on turned William and Mary chairs.

Knobs   Pulls used on drawers and doors of furniture. Round brass knobs were used from 1795-1830. Glass knobs were fashionable from 1815-1840. Large wood knobs are found on Empire pieces. Most knobs were made of wood beginning in the Puritan period.

Knotted pine   Wood originally a second-best plank of timber with rough knots showing. It was used for painted pieces. Today the paint is removed, and these popular knotted pieces are sold to collectors. Many pieces are fakes produced by persons cashing in on the demand.

Lacquered   A finish meant to imitate Oriental lacquer. Lacquered pieces were first produced in America in the William and Mary period.

Ladder-back This term refers to two different pieces. It can refer to a chair having a number of horizontal slats between its uprights. An early slat-back might be called a ladder-back. It can also refer to a Chippendale chair with shaped and sometimes pierced or curving horizontal back bars. These chairs are also called "pretzel backs" and "swag backs".

Lady's secretary Usually a Federal piece but also made in the Victorian period. It is a writing table combined with cabinets. Federal pieces are on tapering square legs and have banding for decoration. Victorian pieces are on cabriole legs with a rococo flavor.

Lambrequin A short drapery design. Examples can be seen carved on Queen Anne legs.

Laminated wood Thin layers of wood glued together with the grain of each layer at right angles to that above and below. John Belter the great Victorian furniture maker used a laminating process to create his fabulous Rococo pieces.

Landscape panel Description of wood grain that moves horizontally.

Lathe-turned Turning of pieces of wood by rotating them against a tool that shapes them. When the term "turned" is used, as in "turned legs" it means lathe-turned.

Let-in-top An expensive detail found on game tables. The top is slightly recessed (dished) to accomodate velvet, needlework or leather, allowing it to lay flush with the surrounding wood area. The top "lets-in" the additional material. Examples on Newport Chippendale game tables inset with velvet of about 1763.

Library table A large table, often with drawers, or space for books, usually on a pedestal. In England the name for any flat-top desk used for library purposes.

Linen press A frame with a wooden spiral-screw for pressing linen between two boards. Fine presses were made in the Chippendale period.

Lip-molding Molding that slants downward in a concave curve to a narrow edge. In a cross-section it resembles an upsidedown thumb. Also called "thumb nail molding".

Lock plate Metal piece around a lock.

Locker The central miniature cupboard in the interior of a desk or secretary.

Lolling chair A Federal chair. Also referred to as a Martha Washington chair. It has a high narrow upholstered sometimes serpentine back and an upholstered seat and usually tapered legs. Continuous with the legs are the turned arm supports that join the curved and shaped arms.

Long chair Another name for a daybed. Examples are seen in the William and Mary period. In that period they were also called couches.

Loo table A center table with the Empire interpretation of the "pillar and claw" table, with a massive center column, four incurved legs and brass paw feet, often used for cards.

Looking glass A mirror. Looking glass is seen on various English Queen Anne secretaries. Not an American descriptive word.

Loop arm A Queen Anne curved arm.

Loop back Another name for bow-back. Example is the loop-back or bow-back Windsor.

Loose seat A slip-seat. Examples found on Hepplewhite chairs.

Loose-leaf Table leaf inserted into the opening of an extension table to enlarge its capacity. Examples seen in Sheraton period.

Lounge A late 19th century sofa or couch. Often these pieces had one arm higher than the other. An example is the American Empire lounge with the back at one end and the arms of different heights.

Love seat A double chair. "Darby and Joan seat" is the English term. "Confidantes" is the French is the term.

Low-back Name given to a type of Windsor arm-chair. The back has a horseshoe shaped arm-rail and short spindles.

Lowboy   A low, tablelike chest, inspired by the English flat-topped dressing table. "Lowboys" are American. Lowboys can be the base or lower portion of a highboy. The Queen Anne period in America produced many fine lowboys.

Lozenge   A diamond shape. Examples can be seen in the form of applied decoration or incised carving on Puritan pieces.

Lunette   This is a semi-circle, half-moon or fan shape. Lunette shapes appear carved and painted on Puritan chests and as inlay on Federal pieces. (usually in satinwood)

Lyre   A decorative design found on classical Greek furniture which used the harp as a motif or detail. Examples can be found on chair-backs and table supports in the Federal periods. Thomas Sheraton was particularly fond of this design. The lyre is one of the most recognizable motifs of the neo-classical period. On Empire pieces it is often used as a table support.

Mahogany wood   A strong tropical wood. Beginning in the 16th century it was used to build ships. It is called the ideal cabinet wood. It has a variety of figures and takes a fine polish. The finest mahogany came from Cuba. Mahogany was used extensively in the Chippendale period. The color ranges from yellowish or pinkish tones to deep reddish or purplish brown. Mahogany does not gray from sunlight.

Maple wood   Group of many species of wood found in North America. Rock or sugar maple was the specie most used for furniture in America. It is strong and hard and has a straight grain. Timbers with markings of bird's-eye, stripe, and curl are highly valued. Curly maple combined with mahogany was featured in the Federal periods. It was used from about 1650 for furniture in America.

Market value   The retail cash value of a piece.

Marlborough feet   A square foot found on Chippendale square legs.

Marquetry   Contrasting inlay. Examples are seen on William and Mary pieces.

Married piece   A piece that may be combined of authentic pieces, but has been "made-up" from more than one source. This would not be a fake if it is properly identified. Some married pieces are delightful. Some were "hasty weddings", and others are "living-in-sin". An example would be a chest combined with an open bookcase.

Martha Washington chair A Chippendale, Hepplewhite or Sheraton chair with open-arms and a high upholstered back and upholstered seat. In England the same piece is called a "Gainsborough chair", after Thomas Gainsborough the famous English portrait painter who painted many of his subjects in such chairs. A Federal chair with a high, narrow upholstered sometimes serpentine back, and an upholstered seat. Open wood arms and usually tapered legs. Continuous with the legs are the turned arm supports that join the curved and shaped arms. Also called a "lolling chair".

Martha Washington table A sewing table with an oval upper part with rounded ends which served as boxes. The top lifts up. It is set on four legs or a pedestal or lyre base. No bag was used on this type of table. These were made in the 18th and 19th century.

Mask carvings Not a usual American design, but some are found on Boston Chippendale pieces and later in the Victorian period. John Belter used masks on the knee and cresting of various chairs in the Victorian period in the 1830's.

Melon foot English bun foot with vertical grooves. The melon foot is not an American foot. They were seen on English William and Mary pieces.

Melon turning A large round turning. Examples are seen on American Empire pieces such as sofas.

Memory pieces Early pieces of furniture made in American referred to as "memory pieces", because they were made similar to pieces the furniture maker had known before emigrating. Puritan furniture was made in this manner.

Meridienne A short Victorian daybed or couch with the arms shaped into the upholstered back creating a slope back.

Milk paint 19th century paint based on skim milk, pigments, and hardeners. Examples are seen on early country pieces.

Mitered joint A joint cut at an angle, generally 45 degrees.

Mixing table   Also called a slab table. Originally simple tables, often with inset stone tops, used for mixing. Choice examples have delft tile tops. They are first seen in the William and Mary period and are very rare. Later mixing tables often had a storage section on two sides.

Molded base   The base of a casepiece formed of molded elements.

Molded cornice   Cornice formed with molded elements.

Moldings   Long, narrow, ornamental surfaces that have a profile that casts a shadow.

Monkeyed   A repair or addition, such as a carved shell, for the purpose of making a piece look older or more valuable. An example would be adding inlay to a plain piece.

William Morris   1834-1896 An English designer whose work was inspired by medievalism. His influence was seen in the American Victorian period.

Mortice   A hole or slot made in a piece of furniture to receive a tenon. This was seen in the Puritan period for use in wainscot construction.

Mounts   The brass handles, escutcheons and plates seen on furniture. This word also applies to ormolu decorations, pressed glass, wooden knobs, as well as lock-plates and hinges. Puritan period handles were elongated wood knobs. William and Mary mounts were brass teardrop and bail handles. Both American and English merchants in their catalogues refer to brass mounts and decorative ornaments as "brass furniture". Queen Anne brasses were cast bat wing and willow type. Chippendale brasses were willow plates. Hepplewhite used a bail-pull attached to an oval brass plate with stamped or embossed designs. Sheraton favored oblong mounts with incurving corners with a molded rim and embossed designs in the center. Empire mounts are stamped brass rosettes with acanthus leaves, with a ring hanging from a post in the middle. Also a cast brass lion head with a circle between its jaws. Also round stamped brass knobs and round mushroom turned wood knobs. Pressed glass and mushroom shaped knobs in blue, green, and yellow are seen in opaque or clear glass. Victorian handles on early pieces were carved wood leaf and fruit with finger grips, mushroom turned wood knobs, rosette knobs, Renaissance Revival strap handles, wood pendant pear-shaped handles on a brass plate and various revival type mounts. Details under particular periods.

Multiple scooping Round scalloping. Examples are found on early banister back crest-rails.

Mummy Headed Therms Tapered male "caryatid" figures", or "Atlantes", which typically had a turban, beard, tassels, tapered trapezoidal body with bold reedings, acanthus carving, and two bare feet. Also called a "Turk's Head". Found on Baltimore and Philadelphia pieces. May be called "Atlas" figures.

Mushroom chair posts Mushroom shaped turnings. Examples are seen on slat-back chairs from about 1700.

Mushroom finials Mushroom shaped turnings. Examples are seen on chair back-posts of slat-back chairs.

Mushroom knob A wooden drawer pull that is wider than it is long. It resembles a mushroom. Examples are seen on Sheraton and Empire pieces.

Mutins Strips of wood that separate and hold glass panes in a furniture door. Examples are seen in Federal and American Empire secretaries.

Nail Piece of metal with a pointed tip and flattened head. Nails have been used in furniture construction for centuries to hold separate pieces together. Nails are also used for decoration. Early Puritan board chests were made with nails. William and Mary chairs in leather were decorated with nails.

Napoleon bed Another name for the "Empire bed"; also called a "sleigh bed", which adapted a French Empire design that had a backrolled foot and a backrolled head.

Naughty English slang for fake that I am comfortable with.

Neo-classic The use of classical forms during the late 18th and early 19th century. Neo-classic refers to the Federal period.

Neo-Greek The use of classical forms in the late Empire style 1815-1840.

Nest of tables Usually four tables that fit together as one or separately. Considered a Sheraton design.

Night table Usually a Sheraton table with a marble top, tambour shutters, and reeded legs.

Notched corner An indentation on table top corners. Example on Queen Anne tables. Circa 1760.

Oak wood North American wood composed of many species. All of these are classified as white or red oak. White has always been considered the more valuable timber because it is less brittle. White oak is heavier than red oak, and grows throughout the eastern half of the United States. The heartwood varies from a yellowish tan to a deeper and redder tone. Oak has a straight grain. The first settlers followed the European tradition of choosing oak for household furniture. Oak can be steamed, bent to a rounded shape, and clamped to hold that shape. Windsor chairs are an example of the use of oak. American oak pieces retain their golden tones while English oak darkens. This can be seen on Puritan wainscot pieces.

Octagonal top An eight sided top. Examples on tripod tables from Connecticut, often with a cup and flared shaft and pad feet. 1790 to 1825.

Ogee A molding with a single or double cyma curve, having an "S" or double "S" shape. Bracket feet with a cyma curve are ogee. The ogee curve was developed in Greek architecture of the 5th century B.C. It reached Boston by the 1750's. Many Chippendale desks and secretaries have ogee bracket feet.

Onion foot A ball shaped foot. Examples can be seen on William and Mary chests.

Open back A chair back formed by the framing and splat or splats and are not covered with upholstery. Examples are seen on Queen Anne hoop-backs, Chippendale side-chairs, and Hepplewhite shield-backs.

Open talon   A claw and ball foot with the claw extending away from the ball. Examples are seen on Newport tea tables.

Ormolu   Ormolu is gilded bronze, brass or copper mounts. Ormolu was a French 18th century detail. It appeared on English commodes in the 1770's. In America it appeared on Empire pieces from 1820 to 1840. Greek honey-suckle called athemia was a frequent motif. Americans substituted gilding for ormolu on occasion.

Ottoman   Also called a pouf. A tufted, upholstered seat without arms. This piece became important in the Victorian period for seating. It could be rectangular or round. It eventually became an oversized footrest. It was often used in the center of a room.

Outrounded corners   The corners of a square or rectangular tabletop where a semi-circular curve replaces a right angle. Outrounded corners are seen on Chippendale game tables. Also called "ovolo" corners. Similar corners extending the full depth of the table to the legs are called "turret corners". Sheraton called his outrounded corners "sash-plan" corners. The Country term is cookie corners.

Oval back   A Hepplewhite chair back shape with a French flavor.

Ovolo   A quarter circle. Examples found on Federal sideboards.

Oxbow chest   Also called a serpentine or yoke-front chest. A chest of drawers having a front which is convex at the sides and concave in the center without vertical divisions. Examples are found in the Chippendale period.

Oyster veneer   Concentric circles of walnut, yew, elm and mulberry wood used on English pieces. Examples in English William and Mary period.

Pad foot   A Dutch foot. A rounded flattish foot resembling a golf club, found on cabriole legs. Pad feet are most important in the Queen Anne period.

Paint-brush foot   Another name for a Flemish scroll or Spanish foot. Paint-brush feet are seen on William and Mary pieces. If no curve exists it is called a brush foot.

Painted furniture   Furniture with paint rather than stain applied to the surface. Not unique to America. First seen in Puritan period on all types of furniture like chests, chairs, and cupboards. In the William and Mary period this trait continued. In the William and Mary and Queen Anne periods japanning was an important form of decoration. In the Queen Anne period are examples of paint-graining that imitated wood. Early Windsor chairs were painted. Country Chippendale pieces were painted. Sheraton "fancy-chairs" were beautifully painted. Shaker and Pennsylvania Dutch furniture was painted. Hepplewhite chairs were often painted and decorations were painted to embellish many Federal pieces. The Empire period used gilt to resemble ormolu. Painted Victorian furniture often in Hepplewhite and Sheraton designs were called cottage furniture. Every period of American furniture has some painted pieces. Painted furniture has a history reaching beyond the pyramids.

Paired designs   A matched design found on both sides of a piece. Examples are inlaid ovals found on Federal sideboards.

Palmette   Palm leaf associated with Egyptian design. Examples found on American Victorian chairs or other pieces in the "Egyptian style".

Panel   A piece, usually rectangular, that is sunk or raised from the surface. Puritan panel chests are an example.

Panel chair   A wainscot chair. These were seen in the Puritan period and in the Victorian period as Puritan Revival pieces.

Paper mache   Molded paper pulp that was used for many furniture pieces in the Victorian period. It was suitable for jappaning and polishing. Many paper mache pieces were inlaid with pearl and were also painted with added decorations. Many tilt-top tables were made in this medium.

Parcel gilding   Ornamental gilding frequently applied by stencil. Examples seen on Hitchcock chairs.

Parisian mounts   French ormolu. Examples found on various American pieces like those made by Charles-Honore Lannuier in the Empire period.

Patera   Oval ornaments found inlaid on Federal pieces. Also called sunbursts. Examples on Hepplewhite secretaries, sideboards, and tall chests.

Patina This is the mellow quality of color and texture that furniture surfaces, finished or unfinished, acquire with age. Old pieces mellow evenly. If a piece has a glass-like finish, cloudy look, or reddish streaks, or all of the above, it is probably French polished. Patinas may not be natural due to chemicals or other unnatural aging effects.

Paw foot Variations of the claw and ball foot in the period from 1810 to 1830. This was usually a carved foot made to resemble an animal's paws. Dog and lion's paws were popular. Carved foliage is often seen above it. In the Sheraton period brass paw feet are seen. Duncan Phyfe was known for the dog's paw feet he used on various pieces. This type of foot generally has a pivoted roller placed in the back and is prevalent in the Sheraton, Empire and Victorian periods.

Peaked arch scroll A scroll, also called a scoop, having a pointed rounded arch, achieving a tent-like shape. Peaked arch scrolls are found on scrolled table skirts. Examples in the Queen Anne period on breakfast tables. Circa 1740 - 1760.

Peanut motif A Chippendale motif, found carved in the shell crest and in the skirt shell of various pieces. Examples found on particular Philadelphia chairs. Circa 1760 - 1770.

Peasant carving Incised or flat carving. Examples on Puritan chests.

Pectin shells Shell with comb-like carving embellishing the lobes. Examples are found on Philadelphia low boys.

Pedestal table Table with a central pedestal instead of legs. Many examples can be seen in the Empire period.

Pediment The ornamental top surmounting a tall casepiece. Some are pointed, some are curved, and some have a broken curve or broken pointed design. On Classical Greek or Roman buildings, pediments were triangular. Examples are seen on American Queen Anne, Chippendale and Hepplewhite pieces.

Peg A wooden pin or dowel that passes through both parts of a mortice and tenon joint to secure it. Very small wooden pegs were sometimes used instead of nails to join parts of desk interiors including the pigeonhole drawers.

Peg-top foot   A Sheraton foot resembling a Hepplewhite spade foot, peg-like, narrowing at base. Examples on bookcase-top desks.

Pembroke table   A drop-leaf table where the central fixed leaf is about twice as wide as the drop-leaves. The drop leaves are supported on swinging wooden brackets. This type of table was used in the Queen Anne period as a breakfast table. Some still refer to the pembroke table as a breakfast table.

Pendant finial   A downward projecting finial. Examples are seen on William and Mary and Queen Anne highboys.

Pendant loops   A hanging circular or oval device attached to a small head and varying in width from 3/4" to 1". Usually found in small drawers between 1740 and 1820.

Philadelphia chair   Another name for a Windsor chair.

Philadelphia highboy   A richly carved Philadelphia Chippendale piece in rococo taste consisting of a chest on a raised base with drawers. These highboys have bonnet-tops with carved rococo ornaments and cabriole legs with claw and ball feet. More under Chippendale period.

Philadelphia lowboy   A richly carved Philadelphia Chippendale piece in rococo taste, being a dressing table or table for flower arrangements, with a flat top and drawers. These were sometimes made as a companion piece to a highboy. These pieces had cabriole legs with claw and ball feet. More under Chippendale period.

Phyfe, Duncan   1768-1854 Phyfe is considered one of America's greatest cabinetmakers. He worked in New York during the Sheraton and Empire periods. His sofas are considered among the finest made in America. His water-leaf carvings are marvelous. See Sheraton period for more information.

Pie-crust table   A circular tilt-top table with a raised and carved rim, that stands on a tripod base. The shape of the top resembles an English trencher which in turn resembles a Chinese dish.

Examples are seen in the Chippendale period. Pierced pie-crust tables are English.

Pier glass   A narrow mirror designed to be hung on a wall between windows, often above a pier or console type table.

Pier table   A table that was designed to stand between windows and against the wall. A pier is the part of a wall between the windows. Examples are found in the Chippendale period. Empire pier tables often had a mirrored back for checking skirts.

Pierced bracket   A lattice-like decoration. Detail found on Chinese Chippendale and Newport Chippendale pieces.

Pierced splat   The back splat of a chair in which details of the design are open. Chippendale chair splats are a good example of pierced splats.

Pierced talon   Also called an "open talon". A ball and claw foot with open space between the ball and claw. A trait associated with Newport. Also seen on Salem Chippendale pieces.

Pigeon hole   This is an open storage compartment fitted into the interior of a desk. Usually the interior will have document drawers and a central locker as well as pigeon holes for storage. Chippendale desks as well as Queen Anne desks have pigeon holes.

Pilaster   This is a rectangular or half-round column. Examples are seen on Chippendale pieces.

Pilgrim chest   A chest-on-frame. Examples are found in the Puritan period.

Pilgrim furniture   American 17th century pieces. Term also used in Victorian Puritan Revival period to describe Puritan style.

Pillar-and-claw table   A table with a center pillar or shaft with three or four outcurving legs. Duncan Phyfe in the Sheraton period produced outstanding pillar-and-claw tables. They evolved from the tripod table.

Pin   A hardwood dowel. These can be seen on Puritan wainscot pieces. The Delaware Valley between 1780 - 1790 also made pinned furniture.

Pin wheel   Decorative motif also called a full sunrise or full fan. Examples carved on Chippendale pieces and inlaid on Federal pieces.

Pinched corner   An indented corner. Examples found on Chippendale low boy molded tops. Also called an "invected corner".

Pine   It is quite hard with a definite grain. When it is finished it is a light brown. Pine was used for lids of oak dower chests and tabletops. Northern yellow pine which was used for these early pieces is now extinct. White pine is called pumpkin pine. It is straight grained and is a soft wood. When it is finished it can be a yellow to light amber color. White pine was frequently used for back-boards, drawer sides, casepiece bottoms, and for painted pieces. White pine scars easily. It can brown or blacken with years of waxings. It can also bleach or whiten from years of scrubbing. Southern pine is a strong, rather hard wood, with a definite grain of clear and pitchwood. It takes a good polish and when finished is a light brown with reddish pitch stripes. Pieces of southern pine were made in Virginia, North and South Carolina, and Georgia.

Pineapple   A fruit motif used as a finial on early 19th century bed posts.

Pinetree finial   A cone-shaped finial. Examples on 1750-1780 chest-on-chest pieces featuring three. One in the center and one on either side exquisitely decorate the top portion.

Pipe stem turning   A turning found on Windsor chair backs resembling a long (smoking) pipe stem. Examples on Rhode Island brace-backs. Circa 1780.

Plank seat   A chair made from a single piece of wood. An example would be Windsor chairs.

Planted   A term describing an inferior piece or very fine piece put in a sale for devious purposes. This can mean an article "planted" in a piece, like an old newspaper, meant to deceive purchaser into thinking that the piece was older than it is.

Platform   A late Sheraton and early Empire Duncan Phyfe leg detail, featuring clustered columns on a platform supported by incurved legs with brass paw feet and casters. This leg design was found on three-part dining tables from 1810-1820.

Platform rocker   A rocking chair with a stationary base from which it rocks. These appear late in the 19th century.

Plinth   Block, square or octagonal piece used as a base of a column or chest when solid to the ground. Examples are found in the Empire period.

Plum-pudding   Originally an English term to describe mahogany with dark elliptical marks. This term was used in the English Queen Anne period and we adopted it.

Plywood   Layers of wood products glued over each other. Plywood has been employed for centuries. Its weakness was the difficulty in bonding.

Pockets   Also called guinea pockets, scoops, and money dishes. These are four shallow dishes seen on game tables for chips or money. Examples are seen on Queen Anne and Chippendale game tables. The English called them "guinea holes".

Pole-screen   A pole supported by a tripod, with a screen at the top. It was used to protect people from the heat of the fire. Many have been cut down and remade into tripod tables. If a tripod table does not look "right" consider this possibility. Pole-screens are regaining favor and are in demand once more.

Pompeian legs   Victorian period turned Louis 16th legs that were often decorated with incised carving, and applied ornaments having a Renaissance flavor, with the largest turning at the top.

Pool   This is an auction word. It describes a group of bidders who attempt to restrain competition, or to raise prices. A pool can push prices up or knock them down. Pools generally try to control competition.

Porriger top   A table to with cyma shaped corners. Examples in Queen Anne period 1740 to 1760. Many from Newport, Rhode Island.

Pouf   A large Victorian upholstered stool usually used in the center of a room. A large ottoman.

Press cupboard   The press cupboard is a two part cupboard with a closed top part and a closed cupboard or drawers in the bottom part. In the Puritan period these pieces have bulbous turnings that were used only on press and court cupboards and a very few tables. Press cupboard is also the term given to cupboards resembling English hall and parlor cupboards.

Pretzel-back   A Chippendale designed chair that had horizontal parallel bars or ladder splats. Its legs were straight. A variation was the pierced swag-back also with straight legs.

Primary wood   The wood which is the material comprising the greatest part or outer surface of a piece.

Prince-of-Wales feathers   A motif inspired from the plumes in the Prince of Wales' royal crest. Hepplewhite used this motif on various shield-back chairs.

Provenance   A written history or pedigree of a piece. Who originally owned it, where it was made, when last sold, and so on.

Prospect door   Also called a central locker. The storage part in the center of the interior of a slant or slope front desk.

Pull brackets   These are located on either side of the top drawer of a desk or secretary, and are pulled out to support the writing portion. They may be called desk-slides. Examples are seen on Chippendale desks.

Punching or punchwork   Decoration accomplished with a pointed tool. Early brasses were often decorated in this manner. Examples are seen on early William and Mary mounts.

Puritan Period   American Puritan Furniture 1650-1690 (English Jacobean was 1603-1688)

   Key Words: architectural, masculine, wainscot, incised, oak

   There is very little Puritan furniture available and most of what survives is in museums or is treasured by families that inherited it. Frequent fires in early American homes destroyed and damaged many pieces. Some pieces, however, do show up at auction and certain dealers handle this rare furniture. Even though you may never buy or sell a piece of Puritan furniture it is important to know how it looks and how it was made. This was the first furniture made in America.

American Puritan furniture was literally patterned after English Jacobean furniture. Early pieces of furniture made in America can be referred to as "memory pieces" meaning they were made faithfully like pieces the maker had known before he came here. English pieces were often wider while American pieces were often leaner and more vertical (Gary Cooper v. Robert Morley?) Although there is a paucity of furniture from the earlier part of the Puritan period, pieces dating from about 1670 can be seen. Remember that Puritan households were very sparsely furnished. Museum period rooms show a variety of pieces in a room but original rooms were extremely simple.

My first impression of the Puritan furniture in the storeroom of the Smithsonian Museum, where furniture from all periods are kept, was that it was in finer condition than many pieces around them. The golden oak chests did not look old or feeble. The tables and chairs didn't wobble and we could have used them to lunch on. Many later William and Mary pieces looked unstable and veneered pieces were often coming unglued.

Puritan furniture is massive and constructed in an architectural manner. This is totally masculine furniture. We will not see anything like it again until the Empire period. There was little comfortable furniture for anyone in this period unless they had a soft squab (pillow) or mattress. The construction of Puritan furniture is known as "wainscot".

The word "wainscot" comes from the Dutch word "wagonschot", meaning a fine grade of oak planking or board. The construction of this early furniture was around a basic rectangular frame inset with panels, the frame being joined with mortise and tenon and secured with square white oak pins hammered into round holes. This is "strong" furniture.

The earliest native-produced type of furniture was the chest.

The old pronunciation was "CHIST". These first wainscot chests were made entirely of oak in a rectangular shape, usually with three front panels. Panel chests are very strong and are the finest made in the Puritan period. The first chests had no drawers. But soon many had one or two drawers at the bottom. The drawers are of side-runner construction. Puritan drawers are never lipped. The legs were extensions of the side of the frame. These "stile legs" are approximately 7-1/2 inches long. Ball feet were also used and were secured with a dowel.

Wainscot panel chests are about 42 inches to 52 inches long. Panel chests with a lid of a solid wide plank are probably American. English chest lids are more likely to be paneled. The lids have thumbnail molding. These chests were covered with incised flat carving about 1/8 of an inch deep, with motifs of tulips, round Roman arches, diamonds, palms, asters, roses, thistles, acanthus leaves, lunettes, lozenges (diamonds), compass decorations (compass decorations are incised circular designs), strapwork (Flemish intertwined designs), and other Renaissance designs already known to the carvers. These designs were not original, but even at this early date, we find "American" motifs like the sunflower design, called the "Hartford design" because the sunflower was found on Hartford, Connecticut area chests. The Hadley chest, which cannot be traced to just one Massachusetts town had the upper section divided into three square panels with two drawers at the bottom. Incised designs of tulips, foliage and other designs found on similar wainscot chests covered the front of the chest. Some, especially dower chests, were decorated on all sides as they would stand in the middle of the room. Inlay is seen on rare occasion on these Puritan pieces. English Jacobean oak furniture, however, was often decorated with inlay of checkered and geometric shapes, like the square. The inlay was made of box wood, holly, poplar and bog oak. English pieces of this period also had inlaid flower designs.

Panel chests were also decorated with applied molding in geometric shapes such as octagonal sunbursts, diamond, box, cross, X, arch, and eight pointed stars. Chests of drawers with applied molding are important in the following William and Mary period with the new brass teardrop mounts.

Some chests had only a small amount of decoration. Some with only spindles, some with only carving, some with only the panels themselves for design or some with only simply applied molding. A classical design the Puritan carvers favored was the egg and dart. This consisted of alternating eggs (ovals) and darts (arrow shapes).

Cheaper pine eventually was often substituted for oak panels. Native walnut was used in Pennsylvania instead of oak for chest frames. Spindle ornaments (called balusters) appeared on chests about 1665 in addition to carving. These were painted black to look like ebony and glued on. Frame chests usually had a covered compartment near the top for valuables. These were called "till boxes". Tills were usually oak. Various chests were made with an outside slide that opens to the till.

The board chest was another type of chest. It was simpler to make and was cheaper. Board chests were not as fine or strong as frame chests. The six board chest was not made around a frame, which was a stronger construction, but simply by nailing six boards into a rectangular box, hence the name "board chest". Board chests, as well as frame chests had "till boxes". These tills were usually oak but later chests had pine tills. Board chests have also been found with an outside slide that opens to the till. "Six board" chests were seldom put together with wooden pins, but with rose-head nails. Gouge carving and initials were often found on these chests. Gouge carving was dug out deeper than flat incised carving. Some board chests had stamped decorations. Board chests were usually a little shorter than panel chests probably because they were not as strong as panel chests.

If a painted chest was planned, tulip wood was often used, not the more expensive oak. Chests with painted decorations were made about 1680. Painted chests sometimes are dated. The usual colors are brown, white, black, and red. Flower designs were popular. Painted furniture is not original to America. Painted English furniture dates from the 12th century through the 18th century. The English practice of counterfeiting wood grains with paint was also followed. If the chest was a dower(y) chest, it had the bride's initials near the top. Chests were also made for men. Chests without feet might be sea chests.

Chests evolved from actual tree trunks hollowed out for possessions. A few of these trunks with covers can be seen in English museums.

The chest on a frame was always small compared with the massive proportions of the frame chest (usually less than 30inches long). The chest on a frame has one drawer and a lifting lid. The drawers have side-runner construction like the wainscot chests. Chests on a frame are often called "pilgrim chests". These were decorated with flat carvings or similar decorations found on other chests. The square legs and stretchers on the frame were replaced with lathe turned legs and stretchers, in vase, ball, spiral twisted, reel, or knob shapes.

By 1690 highboys began to replace the chest.

Besides the chest, Puritan craftsmen made court and press cupboards, gate-leg tables, trestle tables, joined stools and wainscot chairs that were called "Great Chairs", turned arm-chairs and three-legged arm-chairs (triangular chairs).

American 17th century joined stools were made of oak, maple or birch, but the seat was often northern yellow pine and they were about 23 inches high. In England, joined stools were entirely of oak. The stools had raked legs for stability.

The three-legged chair is said to be the oldest type of turned (made on a lathe) Puritan chair. There are two types of these three-legged turned chairs named after the pilgrims, William Brewster and John Carver, who supposedly brought them over on the Mayflower but probably didn't. Lathe turned chairs were referred to as "thrown chairs". Three-legged pieces are more stable than four-legged ones.

The Brewster chair has a forest of turned spindles running vertically to the cross-stretchers, usually with a woven rush

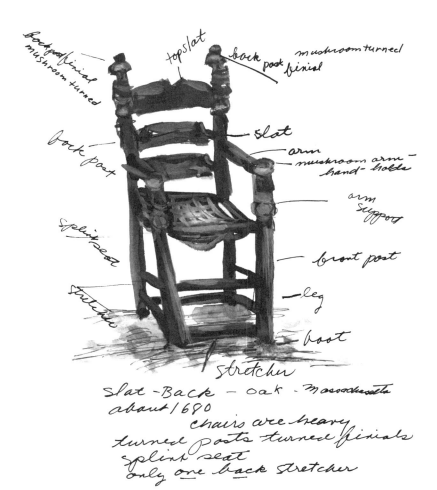

back post finial
mushroom turned

top slat

back post mushroom turned
finial

back post

slat

arm
mushroom arm -
hand- holds

arm
support

split seat

front post

stretcher

leg

boot

stretcher

Slat - Back — oak — Massachusetts
about 1680
        chairs are heavy
turned posts turned finials
splint seat
only one back stretcher

Puritan Table circa 1640

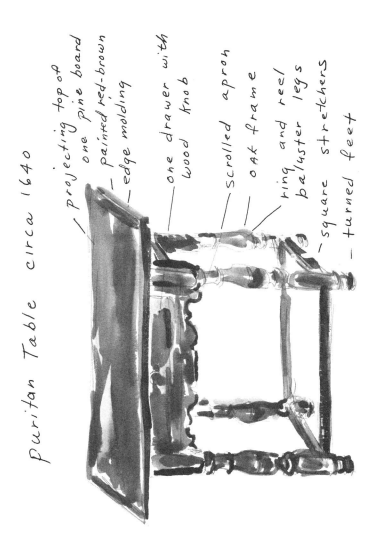

- projecting top of
one pine board
- painted red-brown
- edge molding

- one drawer with
wood knob

- scrolled apron

- oak frame

- ring and reel
baluster legs

- square stretchers

- turned feet

seat. It had two rows of four vertical turned spindles in the back, three rows on each side, and two rows in front below the seat, which comes to forty spindles.

The Carver chair is simpler with fewer connecting spindles, no vertical spindles below the seat, and the turned frame is generally more slender, also with a rush seat.

The front posts of turned chairs were often capped with a mushroom or vase-and-ball shaped finial. Late Carver chairs were also made as side chairs.

Another type of turned chair was the slat-back. This chair is similar to the Carver chair but its back has horizontal concave slats (3-7 rungs) that are scrolled or arched, sometimes with a more important top slat and four legs. The earliest have three broad slats or rungs. Rush was used for the seats. The earlier chairs are more massive than the later ones. Early 1650 slat-back chairs with later added rockers date from the 18th century. The rocking chair is a unique American design.

With a world history of cradles I find this absolutely amazing. This was America adapting English tastes to her wants. Benjamin Franklin gets the credit for inventing the rocking chair. He attached rockers to an earlier slat-back chair.

The wainscot chair is another Puritan chair. Wainscot chairs began as chests with a seat. It was a very impressive heavy solid oak chair with the same character as the wainscot chests. Often the underpart of the seat rail and chairback was decorated with flat carving. Heavily carved wainscot chairs are probably English. Cushions were used on the wood seat of this chair and all type of chair seats in this period. Loose cushions were called "squabs". English wainscot chairs were often inlaid with cherry, black bog oak and holly.

Tables were not common in early homes. Usually a board resting on trestles was used that could be taken apart when not in use. Everyone has heard the expression, "Chairman of the Board". This comes from the important fellow who had "the chair" at the dining board (the master of the house), all others being on stools or benches or not at the table at all. Pilgrim women did not sit at the trestle tables or any other dining table with the men. They served the men and ate later on stools, benches or the floor.

There were plain, rather small tables, braced with sturdy stretchers of straight wood, often with a drawer, nailed together like board chests. These were called tavern tables, but were used in homes too.

Larger tables constructed with wooden pins (and sometimes nails) with turned baluster legs, a large drawer (or two drawers) with wooden knobs, solid stretchers and often with incised carving were also referred to as "tavern tables" or "stretcher tables", or "long joined tables".

Butterfly tables were made in the late 17th century, and continued to be made in the following William and Mary period. The term "butterfly" refers to the shape of the supporting brackets. The edge of these tables was usually slightly rounded. The drawer, if there was one, is wider at the bottom. These tables had turned legs attached to trestles or turned legs with turned stretchers. Butterfly tables with the "wings" pivoted into the stretchers are believed to be uniquely American. These tables are rare and valuable.

Early settlers also made a chair-table with a large round table top. This top formed the back of a chair when raised.

A very few oak, carved and mortised communion tables (about 70 inches long) have survived. If you are offered one for sale, be cautious. Genuine ones are probably in museums.

The trestle table was replaced by drawing tables that were made longer with the use of drawing out leaves. The drawing tables had legs in a version of the doric column, and solid stretchers that were around 30 to 85 inches long.

The most popular table of the 17th century, however, was the gate-leg table. This was a table with fall leaves supported by turned folding legs, resembling a gate. English gate-leg tables were sometimes made of cedar. Small English gate-legs were made in the early 1600's. American ones made in the Puritan period are usually oak or maple. While twisted legs usually say "English", in America rare twisted legs were associated with New York Province, Greene County, New York and the

Hudson River area. In England, frame tables from 6 feet to 30 feet were made for great halls. They were also used for games and were called shuffle or shovel boards. These large tables are English not American.

Court and press cupboards were massive storage pieces. The court cupboard usually had a closed top and an open base with a shelf. Holes drilled in cupboards indicated they were used for food storage. This characteristic is usually associated with court cupboards. The press cupboard is a two part cupboard with a closed top part and a closed cupboard in the bottom or drawers. These pieces have bulbous turnings which are not otherwise seen in this period except on a few rare tables. Court and press pieces often have ball feet. The handles were elongated wooden knobs. Long spindle ornaments are called "balusters". They were glued on and often painted black to look like ebony. Court and press cupboards were decorated with bulbous turned balusters, drop pendants, oval ornaments, carving and ebonized panelings and spindles as well as paint. Sometimes the entire piece was painted. Oval ornaments are called "turtle backs", "eggs", "bosses", "split balls", or "jewels". Applied moldings are seen on these pieces using diamond, box, cross, X, arch, wheels, stars and other geometric shapes.

Sometimes these cupboards are initialed. Often they were decorated only with flat incised carvings of tulips, hearts, arches, lunettes and other Gothic and Renaissance designs the carvers were familiar with. We will see flat incised carving again in the Victorian period which produced revival pieces.

Most of these cupboards were of oak. Some of them were painted entirely in black or red with green for leaves and perhaps yellow for flowers. English pieces in this period (1650-1665) had inlaid pearl and ivory decoration inlaid in these oak pieces. The English also used black bog oak, holly and cherry inlays. The Americans did not. English cupboards often used griffins or other mythical creatures as supports. We used only bulbous turnings. Watch out for Puritan Revival pieces made after 1876. Some are very good. If you want such a piece do not pay too dearly for it. I have seen extremely well made Revival pieces in the lobbies of old hotels.

(Mounts) The colonists usually imported metal products. Local blacksmiths, however, made simple hinges. Their designs included "butterfly", "H", "back to back L shapes", "strap" and "fleur de lis" shapes as well as simple lock shapes.

By 1680 other craftsmen had arrived in the colonies. One was the stainer who stained furniture, woodwork, and houses. The stainer ground his own pigments from native sources or imported his pigments from England. The early colors used were Indian red, Spanish brown, blue, red, and black. Yellow and green came later in the period.

Puritan carpenters and joiners had the pick of choice old trees to obtain timber from, so it follows that Puritan pieces are made from wonderful wide timbers.

(Woods) This period is called the age of oak, and followed the English oak tradition. American white oak keeps its rich golden color as it ages while English oak turns darker and has a coarser grain. Oak is very strong hardwood, and has a distinct grain pattern. This pattern can be intensified by quarter-sawing. On old English pieces you can feel the grain with your fingertips. English oak was seasoned up to twenty years. Americans did not have time to continue this practice but there are documented records that English plank oak was exported to the colonies.

This is the period with no veneers whatsoever and furniture was constructed with the sturdiest woods available. Walnut was often used in Delaware. It, however, was not as hard as oak.

American walnut was more difficult to work than European walnut. The walnut that appears in early American furniture is a light or grayish brown. Walnut has figures of waves, stripes and mottles. It looks similar to French and English walnut but is more resistant to the furniture beetle.

Northern yellow pine which was softer than oak, but not a soft wood like white pine, was used for lids of oak dower chests, table tops, board chests and on seats of oak joined stools. It is non-existent today.

Black cherry was used from 1680 for household furniture. Cherry is a hard wood and is reddish-brown when finished. It is wise to remember that cherry is heavier than maple when identifying which is which.

Maple too was used for furniture. This is another hard wood, although lighter in weight than cherry. The color varies from a light brownish yellow to a rich amber. Maple has interesting grain figures described as fiddle back, curly, and stripes. Maple was also used for smooth turnings.

American poplar was called whitewood and is also referred to as cucumber wood. This is a soft, bi-colored wood of light yellowish and light to medium green tones and tan or brown colors. This wood was used primarily for painted pieces. Tulip wood was also used for painted pieces.

Applewood was used primarily for tool handles, but also for some household pieces or for parts requiring smooth turnings. This is another hard wood. Applewood is light to medium pinkish-tan and has markings of fairly wide bands of a darker pigmentation not unlike spilled black coffee and also distinctive knot marks.

Hickory, which is the hardest and strongest of our native woods with marvelous wearing quality, was used mainly for furniture seats because it was so very hard to work.

Ash was also used on turned chairs. Ash is a heavy, strong wood and resembles oak in its grain. It often splits when worked on a lathe.

Putti   A motif of a child's head with wings. Examples are found on Victorian beds.

Quadrant brackets   Quarter-circle cast brass brackets which support the fall-front of a desk or secretary.

Quarter-round pilaster   This is one quarter of a circular column. It is often reeded but can be plain. Chippendale desks often have quarter-round pilasters that are reeded.

Queen Anne period American Queen Anne Period 1720-1750 (English Queen Anne Period 1702-1714)

> **Key words:** cabriole legs, Dutch feet, carved shell motif, hoop or yoke-back chair, Windsor chair, bonnet-top, walnut veneers

> The elegant Queen Anne style is a transition between the dramatic William and Mary style and the very grand Chippendale period that follows. This is the first American furniture period to have curves that echo the human shape. As a result Queen Anne furniture can truly be called pretty. The most distinguishing design of this style is the shell. The most distinguishing feature is the cabriole leg terminating in a Dutch foot. The most distinguishing fact about Queen Anne herself was that she bore nineteen children.

> This graceful period is refinement personified. It is beautiful, charming, and simple. It is not architectural, dramatic, or grand. Many Queen Anne pieces are small and all are delicately proportioned. Queen Anne is considered the most popular of English styles.

> The Queen Anne period gave us the corner cupboard, the sofa, gaming tables, the chest on chest, easy chairs, bonnet-top highboys and the Windsor chair.

> The cabriole front legs, first seen late in the William and Mary period continue into the Queen Anne period, and will enjoy importance in the coming Chippendale period. The cabriole leg reflects an Oriental influence. This influence is also seen on Queen Anne chair splats. The Queen Anne style saw the leg as one gently curved form called a cyma curve. The legs are short and thick for a heavy casepiece, and tall and slender for a lighter one. The cabriole leg was referred to as a "crooked leg". The bandy early cabriole leg of the Queen Anne period gave way to one with a more pronounced curve terminating in a claw and ball foot, that replaced the Dutch foot. This late leg acquired carving at the knee, often using the acanthus leaf design. The back legs were squared, canted and simple.

> Queen Anne cabriole legs sported a great number of Dutch

feet. Dutch feet are also called club feet. Most important was the pad foot. In addition was the trifid foot which was also called a drake, web, or duck foot. A plain pad foot or trifid foot may be stockinged. This is a vertical, sometimes lobed detail emanating from the base extending to above the ankle. On a trifid foot the carving delineates each of the three toes and continues to the ankle. A horizontally carved top to the stocking appears on some cabriole legs while others have only vertical or lobed carving (also called a socked foot). Dutch elongated feet were called snake and slipper feet. The snake had round elongated feet and the slipper feet were pointed. The slipper foot was popular in New York and Rhode Island. The snake foot always has a shoe. The pad foot may have a shoe. A pointed pad foot indicates New Jersey. The English Queen Anne club foot is more circular than the American.

Besides the more usual Dutch feet, American Queen Anne cabriole legs stood on Spanish feet seen earlier in the William and Mary period. Cabriole legs with Spanish feet often had bracelets of applied molding. Late Queen Anne cabriole legs are found with claw and ball feet that will continue into the Chippendale period.

The distinguishing shell design employed by the Queen Anne period as its major decoration was influenced by the Dutch cockle-shell design. The English refer to the shell design as a scallop. Americans call it a shell. A variation of this shell is the fan. It is a stylized geometric carved half-round with fluted rays. It is usually carved into the piece, not applied. Americans call this fan a "sunrise" or "rising-sun". In England this fan motif is called a "sunburst". In a discussion with James Madison at the Constitutional Convention, Benjamin Franklin described the fan as a sunrise and not a sunset. When pressed, Franklin insisted after looking at many such decorations he could clearly state that it was a sunrise. Madison accepted his opinion and I would not dream of contradicting him. A full fan can be called a "pinwheel". The English prefer a "full sunburst".

English Queen Anne legs often had cabochons on the knees with carved foliage. American pieces did not have this detail until the Chippendale period. Then they are seen on Philadelphia chairs with smaller cabochons. If a Queen Anne leg has both a bracelet and a garter in the middle of the leg it is English. Early Queen Anne chairs are seen with stretchers continuing from the William and Mary period. Stretchers disappear from Queen Anne legs because curved legs made the use of stretchers inconvenient.

Queen Anne chairs are graceful. The backs are lower than the earlier William and Mary chair backs. These chairs have rounded uprights to the back and if arms are present the arms are also curved or looped. As indicated above, earlier chairs have stretchers and later ones usually do not. The backs are curved at the ends of the crest rail, and there is often a concave curve in the center. These chairs are called "hoop-backs" or "yoke-backs". Some have shell carving on the crest rail. Queen Anne chairs have balloon seats and plain, simple splats that were Oriental inspired. Early Queen Anne chairs often had Spanish feet. Late chairs have claw and ball feet, another Oriental trait. Those with claw and ball feet and those with trifid feet might be decorated with shell or acanthus carving at the knee. American Queen Anne chairs are about 39 inches high. Their English counterparts could be taller. The splats on Queen Anne chairs were vase, fiddle, and spoon-shaped. Pierced splats are seen late in this period. The seat frames are generally curved, often with an applied shell carving in the center. English Queen Anne chairs were often covered entirely with gilt gesso and designs of dolphins, shells, and leaves. Unlike American chairs, they could also have Spanish feet on all four legs. English Queen Anne chairs often had intricate carving, frequently of foliage, on the crest rail, splat and legs.

There are variations in Queen Anne pieces. New York favored a wide seat and large knee brackets. Boston sometimes used a compass shaped seat. New England made taller chairs, about 43 inches high. Wealthier colonies used the more expensive claw and ball foot later in the period. Philadelphia is said to have produced the finest chairs, favoring a wide splat, scrolled splats, trifid feet, and later claw and ball feet, as well as horseshoe shaped seats.

The corner or roundabout chair introduced in the William and Mary period stayed in favor and was often made with a slipper foot.

The easy chair continued in popularity from the William and Mary period. It was highbacked and had cabriole legs. It was also referred to as a "wing chair". It was upholstered and comfortable. An open-arm chair was also made.

The double-chair or love seat began in the Queen Anne period. The love seats were stumpy arm-chairs with a high back and cabriole legs.

Some Queen Anne sofas were made, but this piece becomes more important in the subsequent Chippendale period. They had a high arched back with outrounded corners. The seat had a straight front with about 2 inches of the seat-rail visible. This piece had five legs. The front ones were cabriole with pad or trifid feet, often with shell carving at the knee. The three back legs were square and canted. These pieces were 4 to 5-1/2 feet long and their backs could be almost 5 feet high.

All upholstered pieces were comfortable, and shielded the sitter from drafts and fire heat.

The Windsor chair arrived from London about 1720. Windsors had been used in England since 1500 when a craftsman added a fourth leg to the three-legged stool and fixed a bent willow as a back. The first American Windsors were probably made in Philadelphia. For that reason, Windsor chairs are often referred to as Philadelphia chairs. They were inexpensive and strong and sold well. The earliest ones had seven to nine spindles, plain turned legs, usually without stretchers, D-shaped seats, a bow back, and had arms until the 1770's. Windsors continued to be made through the Victorian period. Prime Windsors were made before 1825. American Windsors of 1770 often have downward scrolling crest rail ears. The trait is uniquely American. English Windsors are said to be heaver than American ones. This changes in the second half of the 19th century (the Victorian period) when Windsors in both countries became heavy and complex.

Observing early English Windsor chairs you can see the

influence on American Shaker furniture.

Windsors with writing arms and drawers are uniquely American. Benjamin Franklin is given credit for attaching rockers to a Windsor chair or perhaps an earlier slat-back, and creating a uniquely American piece. Thomas Jefferson designed his Windsor with a revolving seat and writing arm.

American Windsors differ from English ones. English pieces have ornamental splats. American ones have backs made with spindles. American pieces have widely splayed turned legs. English chairs can have cabriole front legs with Dutch feet. American chairs have stretchers more often than English ones.

American Windsors were made with hickory spindles often with pine seats and often with birch legs. They were constructed of green lumber because when the wood shrunk the joints tightened. Originally all Windsors were painted. Most often green but also in red, yellow and black.

Early Queen Anne highboys continued to have flat tops similar to the earlier William and Mary pieces. The first change which characterized this new period was the addition of the broken-scroll top, which enhanced the balance of the piece. Another uniquely American characteristic is the bonnet top. This top follows the line of the broken pediment. It appeared as a solid piece of wood rather than a decorative one dimensional frontpiece. Late Queen Anne highboys besides wearing a bonnet were often a third taller than earlier pieces. The bonnets were decorated with twisted flame finials that were also called blazes or corkscrews. The highboy apron could have three to five fine arches.

Highboys were originally supported by six cabriole legs with Dutch feet, and later by four cabriole legs with Dutch feet, most frequently a Dutch pad foot. The two replaced legs usually showed up as pendants, also called drops.

Queen Anne highboys vary in height from early ones that are about 5 feet 8 inches to late ones up to 7 feet 10 inches. They are 35 to 44 inches wide and approximately 20 inches deep. These pieces do not have stretchers. There were usually six to

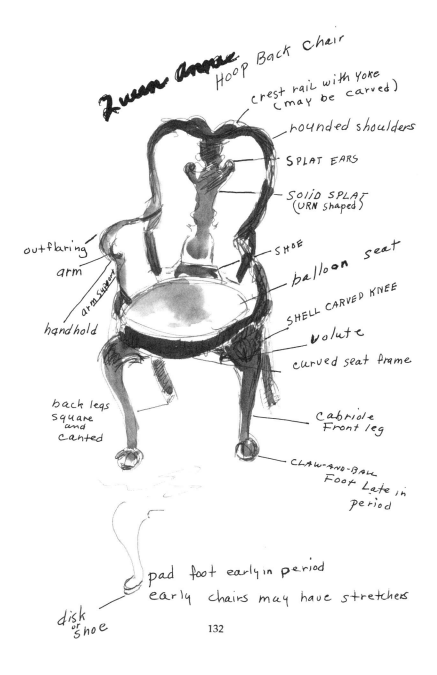

Queen Anne
Hoop Back Chair

crest rail with yoke
(may be carved)

rounded shoulders

SPLAT EARS

SOLID SPLAT
(URN shaped)

outflaring
arm

arm support

handhold

SHOE

balloon seat

SHELL CARVED KNEE

volute

curved seat frame

back legs
square
and
canted

cabriole
front leg

CLAW-AND-BALL
Foot Late in
period

pad foot early in period
early chairs may have stretchers

disk
or
shoe

132

Queen Anne Cabriole Legs

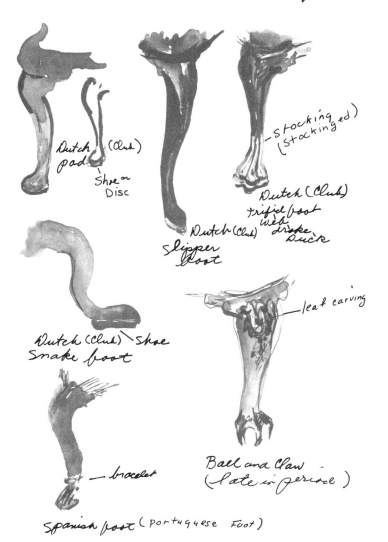

Dutch (Club)
pad

Shoe or
Disc

—Stocking
(Stockinged)

Dutch (Club)
trifid foot
web
drake
Duck

Dutch (Club)
Slipper
foot

Dutch (Club) — Shoe
Snake foot

—leaf carving

—bracelet

Ball and Claw
(late in period)

Spanish foot (portuguese Foot)

133

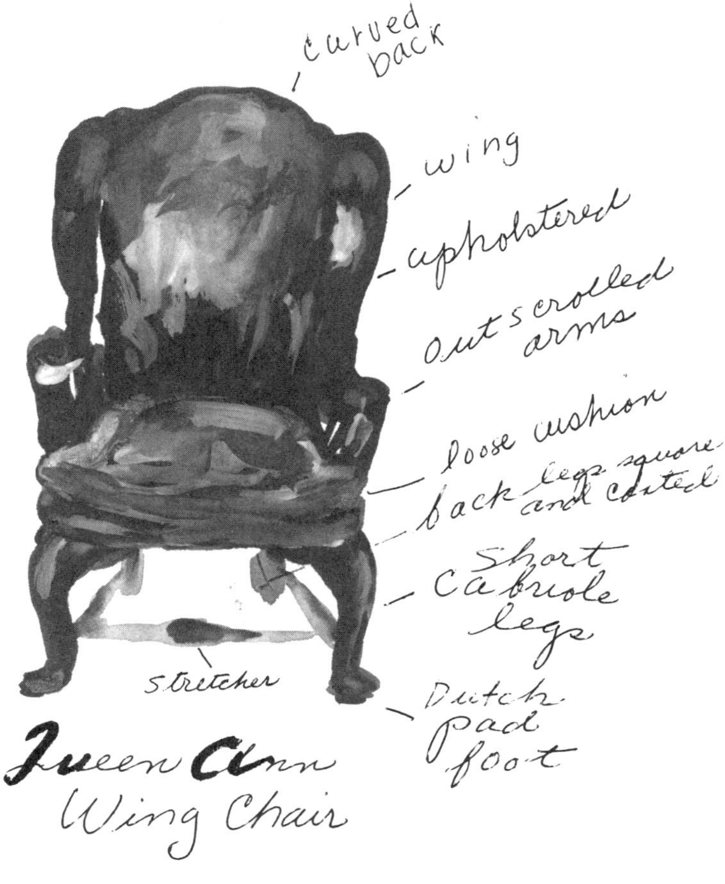

curved
back

wing

upholstered

outscrolled
arms

loose cushion
back legs square
and casted

Short
cabriole
legs

stretcher

Dutch
pad
foot

Queen Ann
Wing Chair

curved Bow

curved
one piece arm

7.
spindles

arm
support

rain
gutter

Saddle
seat

vase and
ring
Turned
splayed
legs

Bow Back
Windsor

135

Queen Anne Brasses 1720-1750

plate

holes for brads

BAIL HANDLE

Chasing and Punching designs

escutcheon

hole for brad

BATsiwing

escutcheon

Plate

Teardrop

circular plate

Scroll edge

Square mounts were set on a diagonal

These are all cast brass
These were all made in England

12 drawers in these pieces. The shell is the principle design used on the highboys. These appear on the central top drawer and the central bottom drawer. The drawers may have arched moldings.

The lowboys are similar to the highboys but the bases are only 30 to 36 inches wide. They have rectangular tops that overhang the body by two to three inches at the sides and about two inches in front. The skirts are valanced, sometimes with triple-arches. Sometimes two pendant finials descend from the skirt. These lowboys may have five drawers. The shell is the usual decoration, but some are seen with quatrefoil or swastika carvings. The legs are cabriole with Dutch or Spanish feet.

The knee-hole dressing table, about three feet wide with nine drawers and a back cupboard for slippers was an important English piece.

Tilt-top tables were important because they conserved space and were easily moved. Socially necessary tea-tables first appeared in the William and Mary period but now have cabriole legs and Dutch or claw and ball feet, and a raised edge around the tray top. Rectangular tea-tables were popular in New England. Tables with extremely thin cabriole legs were said to have "spider-legs". The tripod tea-table with a "birdcage" design appeared in this period, but achieved true greatness in the Chippendale period that follows.

The gate-leg table was replaced by the cabriole-legged dropleaf table. Drop-leaf tables in rectangular, square, oval and circular shapes with leaves supported by moveable brackets became important. A drop-leaf with a swinging leg was also made. Card or game tables favored moveable legs.

The pembroke table was a late addition to the Queen Anne period, but reached its prominence in the Chippendale period. It was originally intended as a breakfast table. The handkerchief table, another late addition, was also referred to as a breakfast table.

Chests were designed to stand on bracket feet or with bandy cabriole legs with Dutch feet. Torus molding can be seen on various chest tops. Queen Anne chests usually have scrolled aprons, five or six drawers, and are thirty-four to thirty-eight inches wide.

The chest on a frame was constructed in two separate sections. The upper part held the drawers, and the frame is the under part. These pieces could be four to six feet high and have cabriole legs with Dutch feet.

The Queen Anne period included a desk-on-a-frame with a slant or slope front. The upper part was a slanted box, perhaps with a drawer, and the under part a lowboy on cabriole legs, with a scalloped apron. The drawer or drawers had lip-molding. Some desks had concave shells carved in the center at the bottom while some had the shell design on the locker and on the apron. These pieces yielded to the slope or slant front with a chest of drawers with short bandy cabriole legs and pad feet. These newer desks also employed the shell motif for decoration. Many were made in curly maple.

Japanning continued to be important in the Queen Anne period. Many of our choicest pieces were made in Boston and Philadelphia. American pieces were blue, green, black and brown; their English counterparts were brilliant vermillion, green, black and brown. Both countries used an imitation tortiose-shell ground. American pieces were lightly decorated with red, green, and gilt. English pieces were heavily decorated, gilded, and had their motifs raised with thick gesso. English pieces added varnish to their ground colors for brilliance. The real Japanese lacquer that was imitated was thick and highly polished. Japanese artists used forty to fifty coats of lacquer sap while the English used one or two. Americans used less and it was thinly applied. Chinoiserie designs used on japanned pieces came from Oriental plates or design books.

Occasionally you will see painted pieces other than Windsor chairs in red or brown. In England marble was imported from Italy, especially for side tables, but in America stone or marble table tops are very rare.

(Mounts)   Cabinet brasses made in England were a light yellow color. Handles and keyhole escutcheons were scrolled plates or cast bat's wing and willow types, some with stamped, punched or chased design work. The bat's wing keyhole escutcheons have almost the same outline as the handle. They were attached by three small brads (tiny nails having no head or a small one). The willow brasses also have approximately the same outline for the keyhole escutcheons and are also cast brass attached with brads. Brasses were kept brightly polished to reflect fire or candlelight.

(Important Queen Anne cabinetmakers) William Savery, Christopher Townsend, John Goddard, Thomas Elfe and Thomas Johnston were noted furniture makers in America's Queen Anne period.

(Woods) The woods associated with the Queen Anne period are primarily walnut, cherry and mahogany. In England's early Georgian period, walnut, and mahogany were very important. Much furniture made in England between 1720 and 1760 was made of Virginia walnut. This Queen Anne furniture is even today frequently mistaken for mahogany. The reason for this is simple. It was often stained to resemble mahogany. Virginia walnut was used for stools, hoop-backed chairs and dressing tables with cabriole legs. One piece it was not used for was the dining table as the boards of walnut were not as wide as mahogany boards.

American walnut was exported to England because English forests had thinned out and the London fire of 1666 had destroyed the city. Rebuilding and restocking lumber yards was a massive task.

American walnut is quite hard and more difficult to work than European walnut. The walnut seen in early American furniture is characterized by a light brown or grayish brown color and is similar to English and French walnut. American walnut is superior, however, because of its ability to withstand the damaging furniture beetle. Walnut bleached by sunlight becomes grayer. Irregular growths, crooks, forks, stumps, and burls yielded prized veneers. American walnut may produce timber marks by striped, waved or mottled figures. Many beautiful pieces were produced in New England, New York, Virginia and Pennsylvania of American walnut.

American black or wild cherry grows throughout the eastern half of America, except in southern Florida. This wood is moderately hard and straight grained. Cherry wood is a light reddish-tan. On some timbers, a mild type of ring growth figure can be found and in rare instances, swirl, feather-crotch or wavy figures are seen on choice pieces. The texture is fine with small pores. During colonial times, black cherry was used particularly in the states situated above Pennsylvania and New Jersey. In New England and New York, cherry was used for seating furniture as well as cabinetwork. In Connecticut cherry was used for the finest pieces, including highboys, lowboys, secretaries and chests.

Mahogany came from Honduras and the West Indian Islands, Jamaica, Puerto Rico, Santo Domingo and Cuba. This wood took less time to season than oak or walnut and boards were often 12 feet wide. This is an ideal cabinet wood. It has rich color tones, handsome fiddleback figures and markings of curl and stripe and blister. The color range is from yellowish or pinkish hues to a deep reddish or purplish brown. Mahogany does not gray from exposure to the sun. Also, the heartwood has a capacity to repel larvae that damage so much furniture made of other woods. Mahogany could be beautifully carved out and it shrinks and warps less than any other wood. Mahogany pieces from this period that were French polished in later periods turn from a natural mellow brown to a reddish tint and often have a cloudy look. The patina often becomes uneven in color.

A great deal of English Queen Anne furniture was made of elm, but this wood developed woodworm. Very little remains today.

Rail   A horizontal connecting piece in furniture construction. Chairs have seat-rails, crest-rails, back-rails, stretchers. Rails hold the sides of casepieces together.

Rain gutter   Also called a seat groove. This is the groove around the back and sides of a wood seat. Examples on various Windsor chairs.

Rake   The angle or slant of various furniture legs. Examples are seen on many Chippendale side-chair rear legs.

Rat claw foot   Spidery claws surrounding a ball on a cabriole leg. More often found on English pieces. It is, however, seen on various small American tables with a cabriole leg.

Rayed shell   A geometric half-circle design formed with crisp straight (ray) lines. Examples on Queen Anne highboys and lowboys.

Recamier sofa   A sofa from the Sheraton period having raised ends. It is French Directoire in design, and was named for Madame Recamier. These were also made in the Empire period and called a "Grecian couch".

Recessed stretcher   A box stretcher with the front rail located a little behind the front legs to allow room for the occupant's heels. These can be seen on Chippendale straight-legged sofas.

Red filler   A finish used on country pieces until 1835. Spanish brown was mixed with raw linseed oil and thinned with turpentine.

Red Gumwood   Also called Bilsted. Red Gum wood is straight-grained but soft and easily dented. It was used for William and Mary chests and kas's. It was usually painted. Few have survived.

Reeding   A number of narrow, vertical grooves resembling small convex flutings. Examples are seen on Sheraton and Victorian furniture legs.

Repairs   This term refers to small mending, not substituting or adding new parts to any degree.

Reproduction   A modern copy of an antique which is acknowledged as a copy. This is not faking.

Rest bed   A day bed first seen in William and Mary period in America.

Restoration   More than repair. Restoration means to renew and return a piece to its first state by adding new parts, substituting parts for missing or damaged ones. Restoration is proper and should be respected because without it, many fine pieces would be lost. Good workmanship is very important. Good pieces can be ruined by inferior craftsmen.

Reverse curve sofa   A camel-back Chippendale piece with a peak on either side of the hump.

Revivals   Designs and styles from previous time periods.

Rhode Island School   18th Century American furniture from Newport, Rhode Island, famous for block front pieces. See Chippendale period.

Ribbon-back   An English Chippendale chair, with its back composed with twining ribbons. This rococo chair design was not made in America. However, in Maryland, New York, and Pennsylvania a ribbon design was made in the American Chippendale period, but not the famous "ribbon-back".

Ribs   Ribs usually refer to curved elements such as those composing Hepplewhite's shield-back chair splats.

Ring and Ball   A turning of ring and ball elements.

Ring turnings   A thick or a thin circular turning. Ring turnings may be composed of one or many rings. Hitchcock Empire chairs have ring-turned legs.

Rocking chair   A unique American design. The Windsor rocker was supposedly invented by Benjamin Franklin about 1750. He is said to have first placed rockers on an earlier slat-back chair. Rockers are about 14 to 16 inches from the ground. Victorian rockers have lower seats, about 12 inches from the ground. The Salem and Boston rockers have backs with long spindles that curve first back and then forth. The later Boston rocker has a rolled seat that upturns at the rear and down turns at the front.

Rococo   Elaborate ornamentation with luscious curves that combined shell, rocks, and rustic naturalistic forms. This rather playful style originated in France about 1720. On American Chippendale pieces rococo is stately. American rococo revival appears in the Victorian period between 1850 to 1870.

Roe   Dark flakes in a mahogany figure.

Rolled-arm   Arms having an outward curve or roll, seen on chairs and sofas. Many American Empire sofas had rolled arms.

Rolling seat   Seat which upturns at the rear and down turns at the front, found on Boston rockers. A very American piece.

Roll-top desk   A desk that closes by use of a flexible cylindrical hood having a convex shape. These are often seen on Victorian desks.

Rope-turned   Turning resembling a rope. Examples are seen on Federal sideboards with three quarter rope turned columns.

Rose-headed nail   Old hand forged nail.

Rosette   Ornament resembling a flower. A circular detail with curved petals. Examples seen carved in pairs on the scrolls of Chippendale bonnet-tops. Also in ormolu and gilt in the Empire period.

Rosette knobs   A wood knob about one inch wide, that projected out about one inch and was decorated with a wood rosette that was about two and one-half inches in diameter. Examples seen in the Victorian period.

Rosewood   Wood from Brazil and Madagascar. The color range is from yellowish-tan to orange and deeper red tones to a very dark purplish color. It has brownish or black pigment figures, and may have ivory streaks. Rosewood was most important in the late 18th and early 19th century. Wonderful rosewood pieces were made in the Empire period and in the early Victorian period.

Round front   Also known as elliptic front, swell front, or curved front. Examples are seen in the Hepplewhite period on casepieces.

Roundabout   Corner chair. Examples first seen in the William and Mary period.

Roundel   A round disk decorative ornament, sometimes incised. Examples are seen on Victorian pieces.

Runners   Wooden strips attached to the inner sides of a casepiece on which the drawer slides.

Rush seat A furniture seat made of tightly woven or twisted rush. Examples are seen on Puritan and William and Mary chairs. Rush seats are also seen on country pieces.

Rustic furniture Country pieces associated with logging areas like the Adirondocks in New York. Often composed of tree parts with the bark left intact. Chairs constructed from branches, sideboards of white birch bark and tables of white birch bark and yellow birch trim. Some had painted scenic panels. Oriental, Hepplewhite and Sheraton influences are seen on these pieces. They were made by locals for resort hotels, camps, cottages and for extra money.

"S" scroll A double curved scroll. Examples on William and Mary cane chairs. Also on swan and goose-neck pediments. "S" scrolls are also found carved on the front skirts of New Hampshire tall chests.

Saber leg Also called a Waterloo leg. Usually on the front legs of a chair, they curve like a saber. This type of leg is also found on small sofas attributed to Duncan Phyfe as well as on many Sheraton chairs.

Saddle seat Usually seen on Windsor chairs, a solid wooden seat with a central ridge at the front resembling the pommel on a saddle.

Salem rocker New England rocking chair after 1800. It has a lower back than the Boston rocker.

Salem Secretary A variety of Sheraton style secretary-bookcases. In New England this piece is also called a Salem desk. The recessed upper portion is designed with two or four glazed doors that enclose the bookcase portion. The projecting lower section is fitted with two or three rows of drawers. In one type the top center drawer in the lower section is designed with a fall-front writing desk. In another type the lower part of the top recesses bookcase section is fitted with small drawers and pigeonholes.

Salted Placing an inferior piece or an extra fine piece into a sale for devious purposes.

Sash plan corners Sheraton's term for ovolo or quarter-circle corners. Examples found on his chests.

Satinwood Wood from the East Indies and Ceylon. It belongs to the mahogany family The type most frequently used on American furniture came from Ceylon. It varies from light to dark golden tones. It is a hard but brittle wood. It is lustrous and takes a fine polish. It is too brittle for large pieces and was primarily used for cross-banding. Some English chairs, however, are made entirely of satinwood. Examples are found inlaid on our Federal furniture.

Satyre masks Mythological male facial design seen on English furniture 1730 to 1740, often on the knees of cabriole legs. American pieces occasionally had faces on their knees in the Chippendale period.

Scalloped leaves Serpentine table leaves. Examples found on Sheraton Pembroke tables.

Scalloped panels Secretary and clothes press panels with this serpentine design on their doors were made in the Chippendale period. This feature usually appeared in only the upper or only the lower section, the other having plain doors. Sometimes a scalloped panel top may have a bombe' lower section. This detail is seen on various Boston pieces.

Scalloped top Table top with serpentine edge. Examples found on Connecticut Queen Anne lowboys and various Chippendale tables.

Scoops Four shallow saucers found on card table tops for chips or money. Also known as "guinea pockets". Examples in the Chippendale period.

Screws A metal fastener with a tapered shank and slotted head. Before 1760 screw threads were hand filed and had slightly pointed heads. After 1760 screw-heads were blunter or flatter. After 1851 screws were machine made. A handmade screw on an original piece fits tightly and will be hard to remove.

Scroll back A William and Mary turned chair with scrolled slats (usually five) usually with ball feet. Later six slat-scroll backs sometimes had the new cabriole leg.

Scroll top A curved broken arch pediment used on casepieces. Also called a swan or goose neck. These are seen on Queen Anne and Chippendale tall casepieces. "Scroll-top" often indicates a bonnet-top that covers the entire top from fore to aft. See bonnet-top.

Scrolled leg Serpentine curved legs terminating in scrolled feet. Examples on Victorian Rococo tables with marble tops.

Scrubbed Condition of pine table-tops that have been worn smooth and are grayish-white in color from years of washing. These were originally kitchen tables.

Seat groove Also called a rain gutter. This is the groove around the back and sides of a wood seat. Examples on various Windsor chairs.

Secondary wood Woods that are not visible, such as bracings, backboards, and shelves, and are not the same wood as the one used for the outside or for the principle parts of a piece.

Secretary A desk combined with drawers below and bookcases or shelves in the upper portion. The upper portion may be closed.

Serpentine front A furniture front having a curve that is convex in the middle and ends, but is concave in between. Various Hepplewhite sideboards have a serpentine front.

Serpentine wing An upholstered curved arm. Examples seen on various Federal wing chairs.

Serving table A 19th century Victorian dining room piece used to supplement the sideboard and usually placed opposite it for already used dishes. In a small room it might replace the sideboard.

Settee A light open seat for two to six persons, having a low back and arms. Windsors were made in settee form as were Hitchcock pieces. The Queen Anne, Chippendale, Hepplewhite and Sheraton period had settee pieces.

Settle A wooden bench with an enclosed back and arms. Examples seen in country pieces.

Sewing table   A small work table. Examples in the 17th and 18th century.

Shaker furniture   Furniture made by early 19th century religious group. It is pure in line and functional in form. Usually it was constructed of pine, maple, walnut or fruit woods. Although Shaker furniture had an English base it displays originality. It is perhaps the most original furniture made in America, but it never developed into a major style.

Shaker red   A russet or ochre-red or reddish-yellow paint used by American Shakers on their furniture. The term "shaker-red" was used although the color varied.

Shell design   Carved shell motif came to England from a Dutch cockleshell design. We first see it in our Queen Anne period. This stylized shell with fluted rays in a half-circle has many names. It can be called a shell, a fan, a rising sun and a sunrise. In England it is called a sunburst. Benjamin Franklin in a discussion with James Madison said it was definitely a sunrise and not a sunset. Madison accepted his opinion and I would not contradict Franklin in this glossary. A full fan (a full circle) or shell can be called a "pinwheel" or a "full sunrise". The English prefer a "full sunburst". This detail was extremely important in the Queen Anne period. Examples are also found on Chippendale block and shell pieces, and inlayed on many Federal pieces.

Thomas Sheraton   English cabinetmaker 1751-1806. Designed in the Federal style. American Sheraton period named for him.

American Sheraton Period   American Sheraton period 1800-1820 (English Period 1790-1806)

Key Words: Federal, colorful wood combinations, lyre motif, urn motif, round reeded leg, splayed-legs, paw feet, Duncan Phyfe, water-leaf design, corner column supports

The Sheraton period is named for Thomas Sheraton, the third English designer to have an American period named for him. He is called the last great furniture designer of the 18th century. He was educated as a cabinetmaker but it is not known if he pursued this trade in London. To earn a living he taught drawing, was a preacher, and an author. He wrote two very important books on furniture design. "The Cabinet-maker and Upholsterer's Drawing Books" published in 1791, and "Designs for Household Furniture" in 1812.

His style was influenced by Hepplewhite who was important when Sheraton began designing. He was also influenced by the Adam brothers and Louis XVI designs. There are many similar pieces in the Federal period and Hepplewhite and Sheraton designs can be mistaken, one for the other. Both fall within what is known as "Federal Style". This period is thus called Federal in style and "neo-classical" in design. This period was enriched by the work of Duncan Phyfe.

Sheraton used the urn in almost every piece he designed. This period utilized low-relief carvings of drapery festoons, bow-knotted wheat-ears, thunderbolts, stems of foliage, water-leaf carvings, rosettes, fruit baskets, flower baskets, pineapples, ribbons, cornucopias, and eagles. His pieces do not have the light fantasy of Hepplewhite.

The French Directoire style introduced in Sheraton's later book used the lyre motif, especially on chair-backs, and acanthus-leaf carving, especially on legs, and carved or brass feet. We see a continuation of these later designs in the following Empire period.

If any one characteristic says "Sheraton" it is his combined use of colorful woods. His mahogany and maple pieces are striking. While inlay is important, it is never used on American pieces as heavily as on English ones. English Sheraton pieces often had enrichments of gilt friezes and gilted legs. Painted cane back chairs were very popular in England.

Sheraton decorated his furniture with inlaid lines, pattern stringing and cross-banding. In this period are seen inlays of flowers, husks, ovals, discs and fans. Stringing was done with holly, ebony, maple, and satinwood. The later Sheraton designs exhibit a Greco-Roman influence (curule legs). Sheraton used very little molding.

Sheraton used Hepplewhite's tapering legs, but also designed rounded reeded legs that are uniquely Sheraton. He also designed furniture with square legs. English pieces are seen with tapering legs having reed carved cup shapes on the upper-most part. This was not an American trait. Curule legs, which are the half circle legs that Robert Adam had used, originated in ancient Rome, and were used in the Sheraton period. These were also called Grecian cross legs and are frequently found on sofas. Brass paw feet with casters are found on these legs and on out-splayed legs of pedestal tables, card tables and dining tables. Sheraton legs were occasionally painted to imitate bamboo. Various Sheraton turned legs wear brass shoes. They are fitted to the leg and terminate in a button.

Sheraton square-back chairs replaced the earlier Chippendale and Hepplewhite styles. Sheraton did not repeat the serpentine shape of Chippendale or the shield and heart shapes of Hepplewhite. The back of the Hepplewhite chair was curved, but all the early Sheraton ones had square or rectangular backs. The later chairs in this period were often painted with floral and fruit designs, and made of maple or softer woods. These were called "fancy chairs". Gilding and stenciling was used. The later chairs had less fine lines and had cheaper construction.

Sheraton chair backs were interlacing rectangulars, often with the central panel rising a little above the top rail. The arms started high on the uprights of the chair and swept downward in a cyma-curve to the supports. Sheraton arms were more curved than Hepplewhite's. While Hepplewhite extended his chair seat cover over the apron, Sheraton usually wanted part of the seat frame to show, but sometimes he imitated Hepplewhite and also pulled his seat covers over the apron. Banister-backs and open-work splats were designed and oval-backs were made, but these designs were more prevalent in England than in America. Hepplewhite spade feet are used on some chairs and stretchers are used on some square legged chairs. Rounded reeded legs do not have stretchers.

English Sheraton open-back mahogany arm chairs sometimes had the front arms formed of a swan's head, with a crest rail of painted cherubs or classical figures in white, often on a blue background. The frames are enriched with gilding. The bent legs are modified saber legs front and back.

Easy chairs were still popular, mostly with reeded legs, and stood about four feet high. Some had curved backs and some had square ones. The arms were rolled. The square legged chairs had stretchers, but the reeded type did not. Some reeded legs had casters and some reeded legs terminated with bulb turnings and sharply tapered rear legs.

Sheraton made his particular version of the "Martha Washington" open-arm chair. His had slender vase-turned and reeded arms and legs. The upholstered back had a serpentine curve. In England this was called a "Gainsborough chair", after the famous portrait artist who posed many subjects in them.

The circular easy chair is barrel-shaped and was generally made in Philadelphia. On these chairs the legs are usually reeded and the back legs out-flare.

The low-backed upholstered armchair was more common in England. It has an arched back and a serpentine line of the arm rests. The legs on this chair can be square or reeded. Some of this type were made in Baltimore, Maryland.

Another Sheraton chair had tapered, reeded, saber front legs, and an open-work back that had one curved slat (composed of two cyma-curves). This type of chair does not have a lower horizontal cross bar. A similar chair was designed using a lyre shape for the back that rested on a cross bar. A third variation of this type had a curved horizontal "X" shape also resting on a lower horizontal cross bar. These chairs did not have stretchers. However, chairs of this type with arms occasionally did have stretchers. Most had slip seats but others were nailed to the frame with tacks. These open chairs were made of mahogany. The Greek klimos chair recycled by the Romans is the source of inspiration for this Sheraton design. Late in the period Sheraton put carved hairy paw feet on these chairs.

The Sheraton period introduced the fancy painted chair which could be simple or simply exquisite. Beautiful examples of these chairs are found at the D.A.R. Museum in Washington, D.C. Some are simple, painted and decorated with gilt lines, others with simply exquisite painted flowers and ribbons. Gilding, stenciling, as well as painting which featured flowers, fruits, swags, landscapes, and colorful medallions was used to "fancy" these pieces. Fancy chairs were often constructed of maple. The Hitchcock chair comes later in the Empire period, but is called a "fancy chair" also. It is not a Sheraton piece however. Painted American Sheraton settees were made in this style. Georgian English painted chairs are thicker with wider designs and are more heavily decorated. There were also many painted chairs in England, during the Hepplewhite period. Georgian (English) painted chairs are thicker, with wider designs and are more heavily decorated.

The Sheraton period produced the double chair (love seat or settee) as all periods from Queen Anne had, but this period also produced it in triple and even in quadruple form.

English Sheraton chairs were often gilded. Some were made entirely of satinwood. Many had elaborate painting with gilt on them.

The Sheraton sofas are American classics. The rectangular form appears in almost all of the Sheraton sofas. The back rail was frequently reeded, often with a raised carved portion in the center. This detail is also on Sheraton chairs. The legs are sometimes square and tapered, as were the Hepplewhite models, but generally they are rounded and tapered and reeded. Some sofas had spade feet. Stretchers were not used on reeded legs. Arms were frequently supported by a vase shaped column. The features which identify the Sheraton piece are the straight back, the arm supports, and the rounded reeded legs. There were usually eight legs on the sofas. These features were used by Duncan Phyfe from about 1800 to 1825 and formed the basis of his finer sofas. Curule legs in the later Sheraton period were found on sofas with brass paw feet and have beautiful carvings of drapes and rosettes. They were castered. Some Sheraton sofas had cane backs, cane seats and cane arms. A cushion was used on this type. The eight legs were reeded and castered. Some cane sofas had curule legs.

Chests of drawers in this period are sometimes referred to as bureaus. They have the characteristics of reeded or ringed corner-column supports ending in round tapered feet. These columns stand away from the casepiece and the top corners are nearly circular to cover the columns. These features are seen in the sideboards also. Chests that have vase and ring turned legs were usually castered. Sheraton used very little molding on casepieces. The Sheraton period also popularized the chest of drawers with an attached mirror. Sheraton did not design separate mirrors, but those with an overhanging cornice and reeded columns with a patriotic painting are called Sheraton.

Sheraton designed chests with elliptic fronts (round fronts) with reeded legs and colorful veneers. Chests in this period have colorful inlays. French legs are seen on some chests, generally with a scrolled apron.

This period saw cabinets combined with a writing table called a "lady's secretary". This piece had square tapering legs, usually with banding and inlaid ovals for decoration. A wider version of this piece was called a "gentleman's secretary".

It will be recalled that Hepplewhite used tambour fronts on his secretaries. Sheraton designed another type. This was the barrel or cylinder-front. It was not a huge success because it was not graceful and what resulted was an awkward roll-top desk. The upper portion had glass doors featuring wood glazing bars, often with Gothic arches. The legs were about 17 inches and tapered. Some had a broken pediment top. They usually had three drawers and French feet with curved aprons. They were never over six feet in height. Sheraton secretaries could have finials in urn or eagle shapes on the pediment. Some secretaries, with slender tapering square

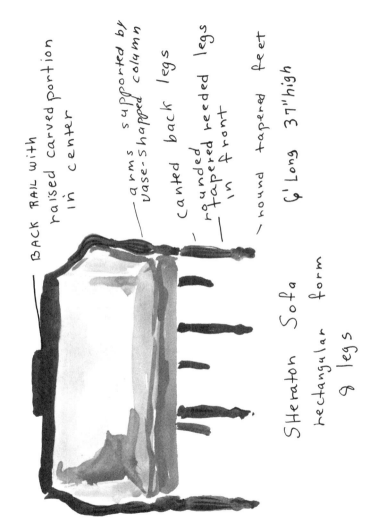

BACK RAIL with raised carved portion in center

arms supported by vase-shapped column

canted back legs

rounded reeded legs tapered in front

round tapered feet

Sheraton Sofa

rectangular form

6' Long 37"high

9 legs

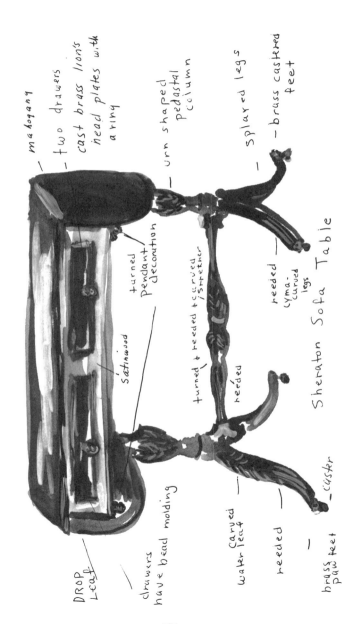

mahogany

two drawers

cast brass lions head plates with a ring

urn shaped pedestal column

splayed legs

brass castered feet

turned pendant decoration

turned & reeded & curved istretcher

reeded cyma-curved legs

reeded

Sheraton Sofa Table

satinwood

DROP Leaf

drawers have bead molding

water carved leaf

reeded

brass paw feet

caster

154

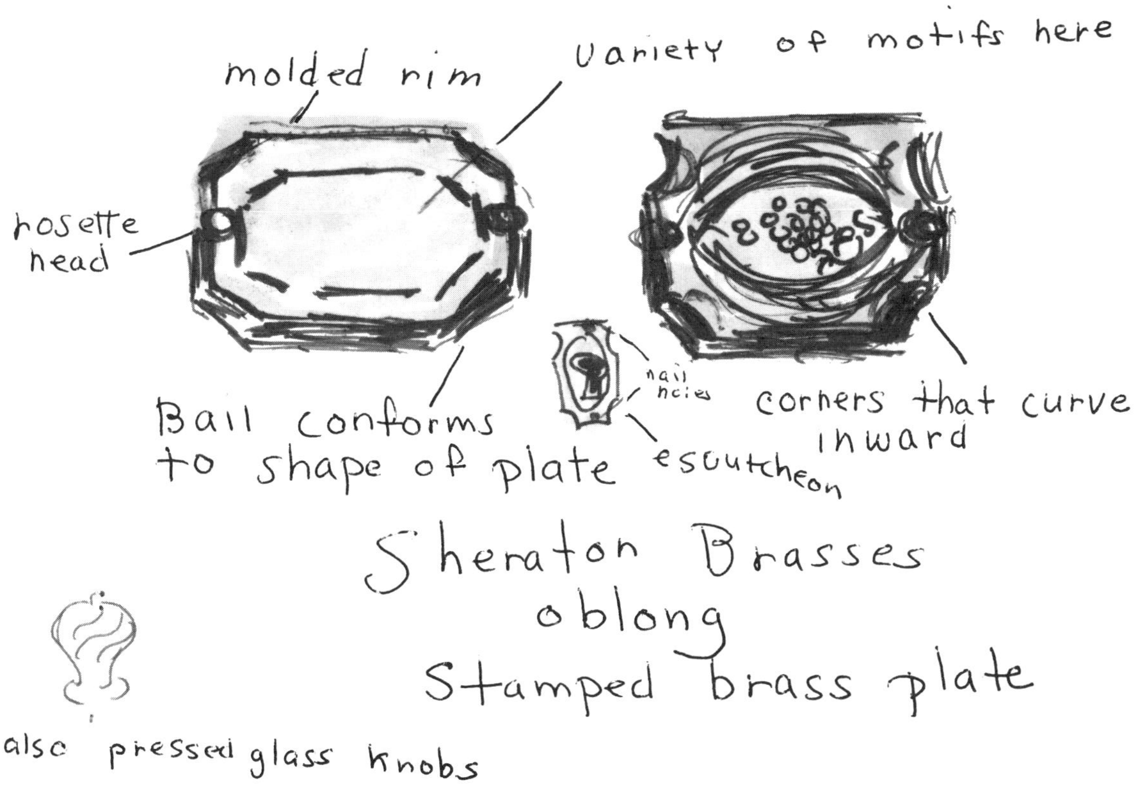

variety of motifs here

corners that curve
inward

nail
hole

escutcheon

Sheraton Brasses
oblong

Stamped brass plate

molded rim

Bail conforms
to shape of plate

rosette
head

also pressed glass knobs

legs, had folding flaps. These also contained glass door bookcases in the upper portion. Stringing was used for accents and inlay is seen on all types of casepieces. American secretaries are not as tall as English ones in this period. English pieces usually have more brass decorations and galleries. Cylinder-fall desks were made with and without a bookcase above with one to four drawers.

The Sheraton period saw the continued popularity of the tambour desk, and card tables were still important. Sheraton designed basin stands with tambour doors and French legs and stands or tables with marble tops with reeded legs and tambour shutters. Some of these tables were round. They have been called "night tables". Work tables for women with one or two drawers, with reeded legs, some in octagonal shapes, are lovely.

The distinctive feature of Sheraton dining, card and pembroke tables is that the legs are generally round, reeded or splay turned if supporting a pedestal that could be vase or lyre shaped. If the table had a center pillar or shaft with 3 or 4 outcurving legs it was referred to as a pillar and claw piece. Dining tables were often simple eight-legged oval dropleaves, with two legs that swing to either side. Some of these tables had square tapering legs and some legs were reeded with bulb turnings and casters. The three-part dining table we saw in the Hepplewhite period continues, this time with reeded legs and casters. These three-part tables usually had rounded ends. Clustered column legs are also seen on tables later in the period, on a platform supported by incurved legs with brass paw feet and casters. These were most important in England.

Pembroke tables are still important with round-reeded legs and casters. Some have straight tapered legs. Tripod card tables and pedestal base card tables are popular as well as the ones with round-reeded legs. Both these types can have brass feet and brass casters. Card tables often have a "D" shaped top. Ovolo cornered card table tops having ovolo corners (quarter circle) were referred to as "sash plan corners" by Sheraton. The card tables do not have drawers. Sofa tables were used in front of a sofa and were 5 to 6 feet long and 22 inches to 2 feet wide. They were work tables.

The distinctive Sheraton sideboard is easy to identify. If a sideboard has one of the following four features, it can be identified as Sheraton. The first feature is convex ends. The second is four rounded tapering legs. The third is columns and legs projecting beyond the body of the sideboard. The fourth feature is a serpentine central portion with a drawer above a wide cupboard with two doors. Sheraton sideboards often have tall brass galleries whose purpose was to balance high stacks of plates. English pieces have circular handle bases. American have oval handle bases.

Duncan Phyfe (1768-1854) was an outstanding New York craftsman in this period. He is perhaps America's best known furniture craftsman. He was not an originator. Since Phyfe was prolific for fifty years, right into the Empire period, he is given credit for many pieces which he did not make. Some are mistakenly referred to as "Duncan Phyfe" when it is meant that they are in late Sheraton or early Empire styles. He worked in the styles we associate with classic revival. His best work was produced in the first thirty years of the 19th century. Duncan Phyfe sofas are considered among the very best produced in America. Phyfe also designed "Recamier" type sofas and settees. The Recamier type is known as a Grecian couch. This piece has a high headrest at one end and is lower at the other end. Phyfe often used a dog's paw on front legs (Egyptian influence) with wonderful curved legs. His water leaf carvings have never been surpassed. The lyre back was his most distinctive motif. His lyre back chair with front paw feet is gorgeous. It is 33-1/2 inches high. His eagle-back is also distinctive. It is 31-1/2 inches high. His pillar-and-claw-tables are exquisite.

Phyfe, like other furniture makers in this time, had his own mahogany yard behind his shop. This shop was near where the New York Stock Exchange is now. The Fraunces Tavern which was close by is still functioning as a restaurant as well as a museum. It is a fascinating place and I recommend it highly.

Phyfe's pieces are treasured for the fine grade of mahogany used. Fine mahogany timbers were referred to as "Duncan Phyfe logs". Duncan Phyfe, along with other cabinetmakers of this time, had agents in different parts of the country taking orders for his furniture. Duncan Phyfe used a great amount of fine carving, turning, reeding, veneering, inlaying and later brass.

Duncan Phyfe began as "Duncan Fife" when he became a joiner in New York. When he became a cabinetmaker, the name changed to Phyfe. Whatever the name, his furniture was wonderful until his later years when the quality declined.

(Mounts) Sheraton oblong mounts (brasses) are found on case-pieces. These stamped brass plates are oblong with canted or incurving corners. They have molded rim and embossed designs in the center. The bail follows that of the plate and is held in place by posts with rosette heads. Two types of escutcheons are used. Oblong embossed plates with incurved corners and a beaded rim and nail holes at the top and bottom. The other an inset cast brass keyhole surround.

(Important Sheraton cabinetmakers) Besides Duncan Phyfe important Sheraton furniture makers include Samuel McIntire, Edmund Johnson, Joseph Short, John and Thomas Seymour, Henry Connelly and John Aitken.

(Woods) Mahogany was the principal wood of the Sheraton period. Cherry, maple and walnut and other woods were used, but most of the finest furniture was constructed from mahogany. Cherry was not in favor in Boston, New York or Philadelphia but was used from Massachusetts to Pennyslvania. Satinwood was important because it provided a contrasting panel against the mahogany. Figured birch is often mistaken for the satinwood it imitated. Figured birch was used especially on card tables and cabinets.

Mahogany is the most valued wood in this period. It is has marvelous color tones that range from yellowish or pinkish tones to deep reddish or purplish brown hues. It has a firm texture. Mahogany has beautiful pattern figures. Santo Domingo mahogany had little figures, while Cuban was mostly cut for veneers. Fiddle-back figures are found primarily on Honduras mahogany. The timber from Jamaica is dark and rich toned. The "plum-pudding" "plum-mottle" mahogany looks like dark elliptical marks. "Roe" is a term given to dark flakes in a figure which gives an effect of dark and light not unlike certain effects in Rembrandt paintings called "chiroscuro". Mahogany is the perfect cabinet wood and Sheraton, like Hepplewhite, used its flashy veneers to their best advantage. Full crotch figures are featured. As stated in the other periods, this wood possesses a capacity for repelling larvae that damages other furniture. It does not gray from sunlight.

Birch finished to look like satinwood was uniform in texture, was a light creamy tan color, and could be quarter sawed to bring out curl figures. In fact, birch could be used for almost all furniture purposes for which hardwood is required. Woods were often stained or treated to look like other types of wood.

East Indian satinwood belongs to the mahogany family and was obtained principally from Ceylon. It varies from a light to dark golden tones. It is fine and uniform in texture with obscure pores and rays. The grain is narrowly interlocked. It is hard, brittle, remarkably lustrous and takes a fine polish. It is generally unsuited to large scale furniture and is used primarily for cross-bandings. However, in England are found chairs made completely of satinwood.

American black cherry grows throughout the eastern half of America, except in Florida. Cherry is a light reddish-tan. The timber is hard and has a straight grain with small pores. In some cuttings, a mild type of ring growth figure is seen and in rare instances, swirl, feather-crotch or wavy figures is found.

Hard or rock maple is a hardwood. It takes a good polish and is light-brownish yellow to rich amber. Bird's-eye maple was very popular in the Sheraton period, usually combined with mahogany.

Rosewood from Brazil ranges in color from yellowish-tan to orange and deeper red tones to a very dark purplish color.

This wood has brownish-black or black pigment figures. It's called rosewood because when it is sawed, a scent of roses is noticed.

Ebony is a hard black wood from India.

Holly is a hard, white wood which American cabinet-makers obtained mostly from trees growing southward from New Jersey. Holly was often dyed to imitate ebony.

Sheraton furniture combined bird's eye maple with mahogany and used rosewood and birch, but mahogany with satinwood and holly continued to dominate this period.

Shield-back A Hepplewhite chair-back shaped like a shield. Also called heart-back. English shield-backs have a higher center shield than American pieces.

Shoe A disk or cushion underneath the foot of a piece of furniture. These can be seen on Queen Anne pad feet. The term also refers to the piece between the seat-rail and the splat. A chair with the splat and shoe as one piece will not be an antique. Examples of both on Queen Anne and Chippendale furniture.

Shonk A large Pennsylvania German wardrobe similar to the William and Mary kas.

Show-wood The wood that shows on upholstered pieces.

Shuttle lunette A design found on 17th century chests composed of opposing lunettes.

Sideboard Usually a dining room piece with shelves and drawers. Federal sideboards were without a top part while Victorian sideboards were designed to display objects as well as store them and had shelves above the storage section.

Side-chair Side chairs, having no arms, stood with their backs to the wall when not in use. So named because they stood originally beside a wall.

Side-table A table designed to stand against a wall. It was made in America principally in the Chippendale, Hepplewhite, and Sheraton periods. It was often constructed of mahogany.

Skinned A piece that has had its paint removed.

Skirt Also called an apron, it is frequently valanced. It is found on pieces above the legs. Pieces with a French outcurved foot have a skirt. Examples can be seen on Hepplewhite chests. The exception is on Shaker furniture with the French foot and no apron.

Slab-table An 18th century table with a stone or marble top. Sometimes called a mixing table.

Slat-back chair A turned chair with a back of horizontal, concave slats. It was made from the 17th century to the present. The William and Mary period produced fine examples.

Sleigh bed 18th century adaptation of a French Empire bed with the head and foot boards back-rolled. It was also called a Napoleon bed or an Empire bed.

Sliding well Portion of a slant-top desk interior (usually the center section) that moves or slides out. Designed to conceal a secret area behind it for secreting coins or valuables. Examples in Queen Anne and Chippendale period.

Slip covers Appear in America in William and Mary period for upholstered seating pieces.

Slip seat An upholstered seat that can be removed. Examples are seen on Chippendale chairs.

Slipper chair A chair characterized by a low seat. Usually an upholstered bedroom chair used for putting on slippers. A slipper chair does not have Dutch slipper feet. Slipper chairs are seen in Federal periods.

Slipper foot A Dutch or club type pad foot with a pointed toe. These are seen in the Queen Anne period, often on tea-tables.

Snake foot A form of Dutch foot having an elongated pad foot, but with the toe resembling a snake's head. These have a cushion. Are often seen on tripod tables.

Socked foot Also called a stockinged pad foot. A Queen Anne detail. Vertical, sometimes lobed, carving emanating from the simple pad or trifid foot to above the ankle. A horizontally carved top to the stocking appears on some cabriole legs while others have only vertical or lobed carving.

Spade foot   A rectangular tapered foot. Examples in Hepplewhite period. Carved spade feet are English.

Spanish foot   A curved-under foot, also called a Portuguese Flemish scroll, or paintbrush foot, found on turned and blocked legs and on cabriole legs. If the foot does not turn under it may be called a brush foot. Spanish feet often display a carved or applied bracelet at the ankle. (Also called a collar, cuff or wrister.) These feet are seen on William and Mary pieces. It is said that the inspiration came from bound feet seen on Oriental women. English cabriole legs with Spanish feet may display a garter.

Spindles   Slender turned pieces of wood. Examples may be seen forming the backs of Windsor chairs.

Spiral leg   A leg resembling a twisted rope. Examples are seen in the William and Mary period. The Hudson River Valley produced beautiful tables with five spiral-legs.

Splay leg   A leg that flares out. Examples are seen on various Hepplewhite pieces, usually on the front legs.

Splint seat   Seat made of oak or hickory strips that are laced together. Splint seats were seen on Puritan pieces. They are also seen on various country pieces.

Splint slat or splat   A slat or splat made of oak or hickory strips laced together.

Spool   Turning in the shape of a row of spools. It was used mostly for legs. It was introduced after 1820 and continued to be used through the Victorian period. Spool beds were very popular.

Spoon-back   A Queen Anne narrow vase splat shaped more like a spoon than a vase.

Spread eagle   A carved or inlaid eagle with outspread wings. The carved birds were usually gilded and used to adorn Federal secretaries. This motif was also inlaid on various Federal pieces. The eagle, a national emblem, was a popular design during the post-Revolutionary period.

Spruce   A light but strong softwood with a straight grain. The grain is less pronounced than Southern pine. Unfinished spruce was used for drawer sides and other hidden parts. Generally spruce is a light brown color and does not have a yellow tinge. This wood was also used for simple pieces.

Spurred knee A curved projection found on tripod table knees. Examples on Hepplewhite pieces.

Squab A loose cushion. These were used on Puritan, William and Mary, and Queen Anne chairs.

Step-back Country term for a cupboard with its upper part set a "step" back from its lower section.

Steps Shelves that resemble steps on tops of some tall casepieces.

Step-top A step or steps above the cornice on flat-top Queen Anne highboys. Examples on Connecticut highboys.

Stick back Another name for Windsor chairs.

Stile The vertical member in panel furniture. The stile is the outer upright on a piece of furniture. Examples are seen in the Puritan period.

Stockinged pad foot A Queen Anne detail. Vertical, sometimes lobed, carving emanating from the simple pad or trifid foot to above the ankle. A horizontally carved top to the stocking appears on some cabriole legs while others have only the vertical or lobed carving. Also called a socked foot.

Stockinged trifid foot A Queen Anne trifid foot with contour carving around each of the three toes extending to above the ankle. A rare American trait found on various Philadelphia chairs.

Stop-fluting Concave fluting alternating with convex fluting. This characteristic is seen on various Rhode Island Chippendale pieces and Philadelphia Chippendale pieces. Philadelphia rococo chairs may have stop-fluted stiles.

Straight front A flat front casepiece.

Strapwork Intertwined designs seen on Renaissance pieces. On American furniture they appear in the Puritan period often on chests. They appear again on high carved Renaissance Revival Victorian pieces.

Stretcher table A large rectangular Puritan table with turned legs joined by rectangular stretchers. It was called a "long joined table".

Stringing Thin bands of inlay for decoration. Stringing was used extensively in the Federal periods. Satinwood, maple and birch were often used.

Stump foot Foot which is not a separate portion from the leg, but a slight outward curve which continues directly to the floor. These are characteristic of Queen Anne and Philadelphia Chippendale pieces. The stump foot is usually found on the rear legs of pieces that have cabriole front legs.

Subbing Substituting new pieces on an antique for repairs or for deception.

Sunburst The English word to describe what Americans call a sunrise, rising sun, fan, or shell motif. These are seen on English Queen Anne pieces.

Sunflower A decorative flower motif that is considered American in origin. It is found on Connecticut Puritan chests.

Sunrise crest-rail A convex top rail in a fan shape and design. Found on rare William and Mary banister-back chairs. A Rhode Island detail.

Suspended inlay Hanging inlay usually attached to a top detail. Associated with Federal period. Example, elephant tusk with suspended (hanging) ring and bellflower inlay found on sideboards. Circa 1790.

Swan-neck pediment Also called a scroll or goose-neck. It is a broken pediment in which the piece has two opposing "S" curves. The swan-neck has a more vertical curve than the goose neck. These were first seen on Queen Anne highboys.

Swelled bracket foot An outward curved bracket foot often found on Chippendale casepieces and almost always on bombe' pieces.

Swell-front Convexly curved front. Examples are found on Sheraton chests of drawers.

Swing-leg A hinged leg that supports a drop leaf. Examples are found on Federal game tables.

Tablet chair   Also called a writing-arm chair. An arm chair with one flat arm that is used as a writing surface. In the 18th century various Windsors have this detail.

Tallboy   The English term to describe a high chest or a chest-on-a-frame. Call them high boys in America.

Tambour   A flexible sliding shutter constructed of thin strips of wood that are glued to a coarse woven backing. Tambour desks were the ancestors of the modern roll-top desks. Many Federal pieces use tambours. The Hepplewhite period favored horizontal ones.

Tang   A wire strip of wrought iron bent to attach teardrop and bail handles. Examples in William and Mary period.

Tassel feet   Found on rare Chinese Chippendale tables, with rococo and gothic motifs. These feet resemble tassels. They also resemble the William and Mary brush feet.

Tavern table   A table with no leaves. It is usually rectangular and has square or turned legs. These tables were usually braced with a solid stretcher. Originally tavern tables were intended for use in a public place. Some were rather long.

Tavern tables could also be rather plain, small tables, braced with stretchers, and nailed together like a board chest. These were used in homes in the Puritan period.

Tea table   Tables which appeared in America in the William and Mary period. They continued to be important in the Queen Anne period, and on into the Chippendale period. Some were rectangular with tray tops and four legs. Queen Anne pieces had cabriole legs. Some were tilt-and-turn tables standing on tripod legs. Tea, an important social function, was served on these tables in the main room. This was not a dining room piece.

Teardrop brasses   Furniture mounts that were made of cast brass and had pendant handles shaped like a teardrop. These brasses first appeared in the William and Mary period. Some were decorated with punched or chased designs.

Tenon   This is a thin projecting piece that fits into a corresponding groove to unite two elements. Found on architectural Puritan pieces.

Tete a tete   Two attached Victorian chairs positioned for courting, often facing in opposite directions. Some small sofas were also called tete a tetes.

Thumb nail   Molding that slants downward in a concave curve to a narrow edge. In a cross section resembles an upside down thumb. Also referred to as thumb molding.

Thrown chair   Another name for a lathe-turned chair in the Puritan period.

Tier tables   Small tables with more than two tops arranged one above the other. Bet they are English pieces.

Till   A covered compartment that was used to store small possessions found in various early chests close to the top. They were made of oak or pine on early chests. Examples can be seen on Puritan panel chests. Some early board chests had an outside slide that opens to the till.

Tilt-top-table   A tripod table with a circular, square, clover-leaf, or octagon top, hinged to tilt vertically. They are never shorter than 28 inches high.

Tip-and-turn table   Tripod tables whose top can rotate as well as tip vertically. The Chippendale period has many lovely examples.

Tongue and groove joint   Used for joining two timbers. On one side is a continuous beadlike molding and on the other is a channel into which the beadlike molding fits.

Top-rail   Top horizontal rail of a chair or sofa.

Torus molding   A bold convex molding. Examples can be found on various American Empire casepieces.

Transitional furniture   Furniture with details from two contiguous periods. This is why it is important to know the major periods and the order in which they appear. The latest characteristics on a piece determine its period.

Tray-top   A table top with a raised molded edge resembling a tray.

Examples can be found in the Queen Anne period and also on block front Newport pieces which have the molding worked from the solid board of the top.

Trestle table   A table composed of a fixed leaf supported by two or three trestles instead of legs. The early Puritan trestle tables were simply a wide board placed over trestles and when not in use taken apart.

Triangular chair   A three legged chair. These were early Puritan chairs.

Trifid foot   A Dutch or club foot. It has three toes resembling a drake's foot. It is also called a duck or web foot. They were used on cabriole legs. A trifid foot could be stockinged or have a bracelet. This was a popular foot in the Queen Anne period.

Triglyphs   An architectural separating device found on Doric friezes. On Victorian furniture these grooves or half-grooves may appear on rococo pieces on each side of an astragel shaped crest-rail.

Trepartite upper section   A Chippendale Newport secretary - desk design having the upper section divided with three vertical doors. 1760 to 1790.

Tripod table   A table with a pedestal supported by three canted or outcurved legs. Tripod tables developed from candle-stands. Tripod construction is very surefooted.

Trumpet leg   A turned leg that resembles an upturned trumpet. These legs were seen in the William and Mary period on casepieces and tables. Trumpet turnings were also combined with vase and inverted cup turnings. Trumpet-turned legs are rarer than cup-turnings.

Turkey-breast cupboard   A corner storage piece made on the diagonal in a wide "V". (breast shape). It has three front bracket feet, two "H" hinged doors in the bottom, two drawers in the center, and two "H" hinged doors in the upper portion. The upper portion may have glass doors. It has a flat top. Examples from the Delaware Valley 1780-1790 with all pinned construction.

Turk's Head   Carved male "caryatids" often turbaned and bearded, best described as "Turk's Heads", found on the legs of a group of sideboard tables and sideboards that are the work of Baltimore or Philadelphia cabinetmakers between 1815 and 1830 on Empire furniture. Also known as "mummy headed therms", Atlantes, or Atlas figures.

Turning   Shaping of wood on a lathe with the help of turning chisels.

Turnip foot   A variation of the ball foot. Some have a collar at the base. This foot resembles a turnip. Examples can be found on William and Mary pieces.

Turret corners   Outrounded or outcurved corners. They may descend to the furniture leg or merely extend past the table top

Turtle-back   Half-oval turned decoration applied to Puritan pieces. Also called an egg, boss, jewel, or split ball.

Twist-reeded columns   An early Victorian detail often with faceted sections similar to the pineapple design. Examples on New York sideboards of the 1830's.

Twist-turned stretchers   An Empire design. Examples on Empire pieces by Charles-Honore Lannuier about 1815.

Tympanum arch   The recessed space between the horizontal and the sloping cornice of a pediment. Examples on Chippendale tall pieces.

Unnatural patina   A wood surface showing the result of refinishing, French polishing, or other unnatural devices.

Uprights   The vertical pieces of a chair frame.

Urn   A decorative vase usually with a pedestal used as a finial or as a finial with a blaze on Chippendale tall pieces. The urn also appears inlaid on Federal pieces often in satinwood. Sheraton used the urn design frequently.

Valance   A valance can be a skirt or also represent drapery. When it represents a drapery, it is often called a lambrequin design or a swag.

Vase-and-ring turned   Turning that combines vase and ring shapes. Examples are seen in the William and Mary period.

Vase-shaped splat   A chair splat with a vase shape. A very slender vase shape is called a spoon shape. These splats are found on American and English Queen Anne hoop-back chairs.

Veneer   A thin layer of wood glued to a base wood. Veneer is also called "thin skin". First seen in the William and Mary period. Many veneered pieces can be found in the American Empire period.

Venture furniture   Furniture made for speculation and sold in places far from origin.

Vernacular furniture   Term used to describe furniture imitating high style pieces with features already out of date.

Victorian period   American 1840-1910 (English 1830-1900)

KeyWords: revivals, Renaissance, rococo, laminating, patent furniture, carved, lavish, rosewood, blackwalnut, variety

The Victorians wanted it all. Queen Anne constancy was not for them. Robust excess was the order of the day. Collecting and collections were for everyone. Victorians used the expression of "going creative". This could mean a different style or period in every room, with Chinese screens, large center tables, paper-mache pianos inlaid with mother of pearl, Egyptian pedestals, Turkish inlaid tables, and fringed chairs. Magazines like "Arts and Decoration" discussed the various combinations and women who had little previous experience choosing furniture relied heavily on these articles. Previously the "man of the house" directed home furnishing. A Victorian home might have Gothic pieces in the front hall, rococo furniture in the parlor, Renaissance in the dining room, Elizabethan in the children's' room, Louis XVI in the master bedroom, Greek in the library, and Turkish in the spare room. Variety was the spice of Victorian life.

Victorian furniture had many charms. One of the charms was that it was affordable. Another was that the deeply tufted seating pieces were very comfortable. Perhaps another charm was that this was the "first time" for many American women, who previously had not chosen furniture. Husbands had purchased the house and ordered the furnishings. Perhaps another charm was that this unlike American furniture made Americans feel part of the whole world by bringing many foreign styles into their homes.

Factories had sprung up to produce furniture. These new establishments might have employed as many as two hundred workers. The large ones had woodworking machinery, general workshops, upholstery rooms, stone and marble cutting shops, and storage areas for lumber, mounts and general hardware. They also had showrooms and traveling salesmen. Their furniture was shipped to different parts of the country. The owner of the factory usually designed his own furniture. (Remember the 1950's when builders designed their own houses?)

American Victorian furniture recycled designs based on all periods. The earliest pieces were a continuation of the Empire period. Victorian furniture was also influenced by English Jacobean, English Gothic, English Elizabethan, French Louis XVI, Rococo, Italian Renaissance, Greek, Egyptian, and Japanese designs. Japanning that had thrilled the William and Mary colonists was also back. Japanese style appealed to the esoteric.

Victorian pieces have worked their way back into American hearts again. Young people scout shops for the huge beds, oak tables, and eccentric chairs. This fantasy furniture is irresistable to yet another generation of Americans.

In England Victorian pieces were more heavily carved, very large, and highly decorated. Hugh architectural Gothic pieces were produced for libraries, churches, the Houses of Parliament, and even for homes. Massively carved upholstered pieces with cavern-deep buttoning, and paper mache "everything" were inlaid with mother-of-pearl and decorated with additional painting and gilding. Heavy gilding and a plethora of machine made turnings enjoyed popularity. Even the simple Windsor expanded to become large, clumsy, complex and top-heavy.

French pieces were also large, and had scads of marquetry

and boulle work. These French pieces usually had finer craftsmanship than their American counterparts. They were enriched with large amounts of brass, inlay, gilt, plaques, porcelain plaques, colored inlay and carving. As usual, American pieces were simpler than their English and French counterparts.

There were many different types of decoration and motiffs in this period. Decoration included scrolls, crestings, cartouche shaped medallions, incised carving, high-relief carving of stags, fishes, rabbits, masks, birds, and dogs, veneering, marquetry, solid wood, geometric shapes, naturalistic flowers, fruits, vines and blossom shapes, laminating, gilding and painting. All these designs came from previous periods and styles.

In some cases several styles are on a single piece. A brief rundown of Revival influences would include:

1820-50 - Gothic Influence
In England, Gothic revival was more popular than Elizabethan revival. This held true in America also. Gothic featured pointed and rounded arches, octagon shaped columns, tudor roses, trefoils and carving. Gothic hall and library pieces were in demand. Gothic styles were also important in church furnishings.

1840's - Elizabethan Influences
Elizabethan revival emphasized ball and spiral turnings, carved foliage and flowers. Chairs have high open backs filled with these designs.

1840-65 - French Rococo Louis XV Influences
Rococo had "C" and "S" naturalistic curves, scroll feet, cabriole legs, deep carving, fancy skirts, flowers, leaves, grapes, acorns, and shells. "Belter" furniture is a good American example of rococo style.

1865-1890's - Louis XVI and Neo-Greek Influences
Louis XVI is characterized by porcelain, ormolu, plaques, ebonized wood, ivory inlay, urns, wreaths, lyres, panels of contrasting woods, classical moldings and columns. These pieces always look "foreign".

Neo-Greek meant pilasters, scrolls, Greek keys, animal feet, scroll feet, honeysuckle and incised carving with gilt enrichments.

1850-85 - Renaissance Influences
Renaissance revival included masks, acanthus, scrolls, flowers, game birds, pediments, cabochons, columns, brackets, marquetry, cartouches, turnings and incised carving.

1880's - Jacobean Influences
Jacobean was strap work, intertwined designs, similar to that seen on Puritan pieces, massive architectural pieces, and oak wood.

1876 - 1900 Japanese Influences
Japanese influences included screens, bamboo, imitation bamboo, lacquered cabinets, Oriental embroideries and fretwork panels.

Typical early American Victorian side chairs are graceful and not heavy. This follows the pattern set by Empire side chairs that were also graceful. They usually have curved backs with the top-rail carved and the splat arched and carved. The seat is rectangular and has a slightly serpentined carved apron, slender cabriole front legs and square slightly curved back legs. These reverse curved back legs kept later top-heavy Victorian chairs from tipping backwards. The Louis XV influence is reflected in these chairs.

Another type of side chair using Gothic design had a pointed arch back and pierced slats in Gothic arch shapes with saber legs similar to Empire chairs. Various Gothic type chairs also have applied ornaments. Other chairs with rococo shaped backs and spirally turned legs or simple turned legs or cabriole legs are seen. These are usually castered.

Many armchairs show the Louis XV influence with their oval upholstered backs that display carving at the apex of the oval. The oval is supported with uprights and the arms are open or upholstered. Open arms can have arm pads. The seat is rectangular similar to the side chair. The French whorl foot is often seen on the front cabriole legs and the curved apron is usually carved. Casters often are used on these chairs.

The Renaissance influenced chair had a keystone motif on the crest-rail and incised carving on the frame and Pompeian legs. Pompeian legs are Louis XVI turned legs with applied ornamentation. There is often a rather large round turning at the top of these legs. Back legs have a reverse curve. This type of chair may have demi-arms.

The rococo armchair has "C" scrolls, scrolled knuckles, whorl feet, cabriole legs, heavy carving, and casters. This type often had an important crest perhaps with a cabochon in the center. The LouisXVI upholstered arm-chair had a continuous concave molding cut into the frame called a "finger roll", with a tufted back, a carved chest, and short cabriole legs. The Elizabethan type chair with a totally open-carved back, usually stood on spirally turned or ball turned legs. The Roman inspired curule type chair was heavily carved. The curule legs were also called "Grecian Cross" legs. Piano stools were also made with curule legs. The Egyptian arm chair often had winged sphinx heads, winged orbs, palmetto, lion paw feet, lotus, gilt, bronze and ebonized wood. This was an exotic piece!

This period produced patented folding and reclining chairs.

The most familiar Victorian chair has a medallion or balloon back, that is deeply tufted, with a seat that is round at the back, serpentine at the front, with cabriole legs, whorl feet, casters, and was upholstered in velvet.

Early Victorian sofas are graceful and very lovely. For a generation that grew up with "family room furniture" these pieces are now cherished. American Victorian sofas were greatly influenced by Louis XV styles. The rococo sofa lived happily in Victorian living rooms. These 5 to 6-1/2 feet long pieces have ornately carved serpentine backs or medallion backs. The backs are rather high, tufted and have scrolled arched crest rails that are molded and have carving in the center. The ends are rounded and the arms are scrolled and supported by arm stumps which lead into the front legs. These pieces have an apron or skirt that is also carved at the center and cabriole front legs that were castered and plain back legs that were canted.

There were Louis XVI style sofas that were very simple. They had straight backs that curved concavely at the ends. They were framed in wood, with the back in one rectangular shape and the seat in another. This piece had open arms with upholstered arm pads and simple turned legs on casters. The back rail had two simple finials, one at each end. These often had brass stringing and they could be painted. The upholstering is without tufting. The single-end sofa is typically Victorian with a high back at one end tapering away to the open end.

Renaissance style sofas have angular shapes, turned Roman legs, triangular drops on the curved skirt, a crest in the center of the central portion of the back rail, incised carving, tufting on the upholstered back, tassel projections around the crest, and figures perhaps on the arm stumps. The Renaissance style arm chair had the same characteristics.

Console tables with marble tops appear with aprons having scalloped shapes. Center tables were round or cartouche shaped, topped with marble or wood, with a skirt shaped to follow the top, usually with carved cabriole legs, with simple or scrolled feet. They were often braced with a curved cross stretcher, often with a finial on the center of the stretcher. Some have cluster-column legs. These were up to 36 inches in diameter.

Many tables were Renaissance influenced. Pedestal tables, with four legs and a turned drop on the central supporting column, and decorated with incised carving on the legs and column show this influence. There are variations of this table with 8 sided tops, rectangular tops, round, and even drop-leaf tops. Most of these tables were made of walnut, decorated with incised carving and had castered feet.

Tilt-top tables have remained popular since they were first introduced. Many were lacquered in black or made in paper mache with pearl inlay and painted decoration. Drop-leaf tables appear in all major revival styles.

The new extension table with removable leaves, heavy turned legs, and casters was used for dining. Later dining tables in the "Eastlake" style often had pedestal bases, square extensions, incised carving, and applied ornaments.

The rococo designs of John Belter emerge as an exceptional achievement. Belter worked in New York from 1844 to 1863, designing, and producing marvelous furniture using his own laminating process. Rococo furniture such as Belter pieces were always expensive, and were usually heavier than earlier Empire pieces. Solid curving designs and balloon shaped backs, decorated with high-carving of fruit, vines, flowers, and naturalistic forms are characteristic of his work. He designed parlor and bedroom sets. Rosewood was his medium.

Casepieces in the Victorian period often had curving, serpentine fronts and bracket feet with marble tops. Many casepieces were revival or transitional Empire casepieces and had scrolled supports and overhanging tops.

There were simple bedroom dressers with attached mirrors, small bracket feet with no carving but with beautiful veneers and perhaps a white marble top. Not all Victorian pieces are ornate!

The Victorian secretary is built in one piece. This characteristic is unique! The piece is French influenced. The top portion is of solid wood, and contains a writing flap that drops down. The lower portion is an enclosed cupboard that also has solid doors. The base has a scrolled apron and plain or carved whorl feet. This piece has applied molded panels. They are easily mistaken for French cabinets.

By 1865 large cabinets in the Renaissance style were heavily carved with medallions, cabochons, marquetry and with heavy finials. These pieces had marble tops, with cupboards in the lower section. If they had an upper portion it was composed of a carved back with a shelf that was supported by carved columns. Other Renaissance cabinets with no upper portions are seen with gilt cherubs, ornamental brass, incised carving, painted enamel or porcelain plaques, and with Ionic capitals. These were called "French cabinets".

Victorian Renaissance sideboards were about seven feet tall, approximately five feet wide, with marble tops, applied moldings, and mirrors surrounded with carving, often with a cabochon in the center and often with additional applied ornaments. Veneered panels featuring burl were also found on this type of piece.

Etagere's or "whatnots" are seen in every style. Collections were put together to display in them. The rococo and Renaissance style pieces were decorated with baroque scrolling, open carving, flat carving, fret-work, finials, pierced panels, applied roundels, inset mirrors, and could be over seven feet tall. Many were designed as corner pieces. Often a drawer was placed at the base. The more ordinary, less expensive whatnots were rectangular stands, often with graduating shelves. Some of these also had a drawer at the base. Many were designed as corner pieces.

There were some lightweight pieces. Between 1850-1860 ladies' fall-front desks usually of rosewood, looking very French on thin cabriole legs, with gently curving carved aprons and a pierced pediment, embellished with urn finials, appeared. These are delicate pieces. Ladies' writing cabinets, also of rosewood, but without a fall-front are delicate.

Matching parlor and bedroom sets became popular in this period. Seven piece suites continue to be important in the 1870's. Beds became huge, some with putti (head of a winged child), scrolls, keystone motifs, laminated curves and carved leaves.

If you believe that more is best you will love the late Victorian period. Every preceding period had influences, but late Victorian recycled practically every previous period and many designs may appear on a single piece. This is "showy" furniture and certainly conversation pieces.

From the Empire period America had been influenced by French styles as well as English. Furniture had grown massive, elaborate and less and less graceful with burled veneered panels, gilding, carving, and ornamental knobs. Change, however, was coming. The late Victorian period produced a light chair, called a "flying chair". People tired of

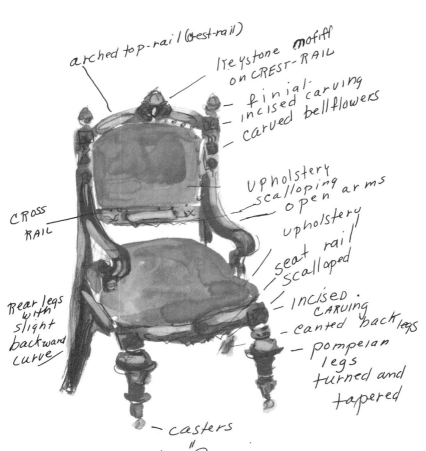

arched top-rail (crest-rail)

Keystone motiff on CREST-RAIL
- finial
- incised carving
- carved bellflowers

upholstery
scalloping open arms

CROSS RAIL

upholstery
seat rail scalloped

- incised CARVING
- canted back legs
- pompeian legs turned and tapered

Rear legs with slight backward curve

- casters

Victorian "Renaisance Revivial" Armchair
Louis XVI influence
1860 -1875

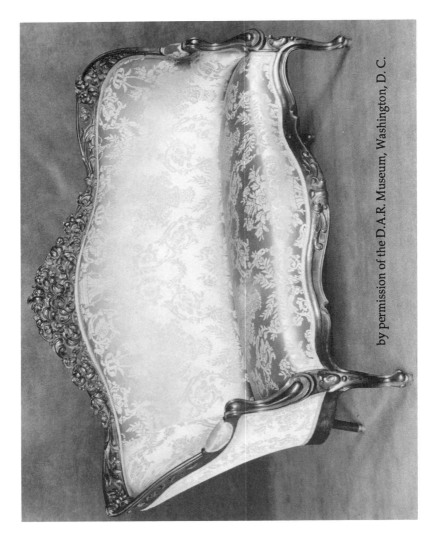

Victorian rococo sofa. Louis XV influence. A high ornately carved serpentine back composed of naturalistic flowers and leaves. The apron is also serpentined and carved. The molding is concave "finger-roll". The ends are rounded and the arms with arm pads are scrolled and supported by arm stumps which lead into the front cabriole legs with whole feet. The back legs are square and slightly canted.

"suites", and furniture began to be arranged to look unarranged.

The name "Eastlake" is associated with Victorian furniture, but he did not design furniture. Charles Eastlake was an English author who wrote about taste in furnishings. His book, "Hints on Household Taste" came out in 1878 and merchants capitalized on his popularity and called their furniture "Eastlake Style". The "Eastlake Look" was a combination of late Victorian furniture made in solid wood, mixed with medieval design, complete with iron locks and handles. Brown marble tops may appear on Eastlake style tables. Eastlake himself was not pleased with having his name used on this machine made furniture.

Furniture in the Japanese style was "in", and the "cultured" took this Oriental flavor to their Victorian hearts. Artists like James Whistler and Mary Cassat used this influence in many of their paintings.

Merchants were selling cabriole legged over-stuffed furniture well into the 1880's, but the Arts and Crafts Movement was building up a head of steam. John Ruskin and William Morris were disciples of this movement. Again English outlook was influencing American taste concerning furniture design.

(Mounts) Victorian handles on early pieces were machine carved wooden leaf and wooden fruit with finger grips behind the lower part. They were four to seven inches long, were attached to the piece with screws and were made of black walnut, rosewood, or cherry. Brass keyhole surrounds were used on pieces with these mounts. Examples of these were found on Renaissance and Louis XV styles.

Mushroom-turned wood knobs were used on various casepieces and were 1 inch wide to 2-1/2 inches wide. Rosette knobs were also used. These consisted of a wood knob about one inch wide, that projected out about one inch, and was decorated with a wood rosette that was about 2-1/2 inches in diameter. Examples can be seen on Louis XV and Renaissance styles.

Wood carved handles that look like straps that were six to eight inches long, attached with screws and made of black walnut were used on Renaissance type pieces.

On Eastlake pieces brass pendant-ring handles about 1-1/2 inches long on a square or round plate and bail-handles made of brass on rectangular plates with chased details about three to four inches wide. Also on Eastlake type pieces is the pendant pear-shaped handle. This has a wood pendant and a brass rosette plate that was chased as well as the keyhole escutcheon.

(Important Victorian cabinetmakers) Some important furniture makers in the American Victorian period were John Belter, Elijah Galusha, Charles Baudouine, Thomas Brooks, Prudent Mallard, Joseph Meeks, John Needles, Alexander Roux and Anthony Quervelle.

(Woods) The major woods used in the Victorian period were rosewood, black walnut, some mahogany and oak late in the period.

Rosewood is a hard, brittle, fine grained wood. It takes a high polish. When it is finished, it has a red-purplish hue and occasionally it has ivory streaks. It comes from Brazil. John Belter in the Victorian period created masterpieces in laminated rosewood.

Walnut is a strong wood with a fine texture, beautiful grain and sometimes has a curly grain. It varies from a reddish brown to a coffee brown. Victorian black walnut was achieved by treating the timber with a stain or acid wash before varnishing. This obliterated the reddish tinge.

American oak is a strong hardwood with a distinctive grain pattern. It keeps its rich golden color as it ages.

Volute A spiral ornamental scroll. Examples can be seen on Windsor chair ears. Also on Queen Anne knee-blocks on pieces like tea tables.

Volute ears Scroll carved ears. Examples can be seen on Chippendale chairs and on Windsor chairs. A Windsor with downturned scrolling crest-rail ears (volutes) are uniquely American.

Wainscot furniture   Furniture built with a frame inset with panels. This is architectural furniture. Puritan furniture used wainscot construction.

Wall furniture   All furniture designed to stand against a wall. Examples are secretaries, highboys and bookcases.

Walnut   Wood used for all types of American furniture. American walnut is considered superior to European walnut, because it can withstand the furniture beetle. American walnut is moderately hard and is more difficult to work with than European. This timber has markings of stripe, and mottle. Irregular growths, crooks, forks, stumps, and burls produced prized veneers. The walnut we see on early American pieces is light brown or grayish brown. Many fine walnut pieces were produced in New York, New England, New Jersey and Pennsylvania.

Martha Washington chair   A Chippendale and Federal style chair with a high upholstered back and open arms. It is so named because of its association with Martha Washington. It was made in the Hepplewhite and Sheraton periods. In England a chair very like it, is called a "Gainsborough chair". The English portrait painter Gainsborough painted many subjects in this type of chair. If you stop at Israel Sack in New York and see one, it is a Martha Washington type chair. If you go down one floor to Malcom Franklin, you would discuss a Gainsborough chair.

Martha Washington table   A Federal sewing or work table so named because of its association with Martha. It was fitted with an interior for sewing accessories. It was made in Hepplewhite, Sheraton and Empire styles.

Waterleaf   An ornamental design derived from a laurel leaf. Examples are seen carved on Sheraton pieces. Duncan Phyfe in the Sheraton period is said to have carved the finest examples.

Web foot   This is a Dutch or club type foot. Also called a trifid, duck, and drake foot. Could be stockinged. Important in the Queen Anne period.

Whatnot Open shelves for bric-a-brac, often carved, and important in the Victorian period. The French word is "etagere". Also made as a corner piece. May have a bottom drawer.

Wheat ears An ornamental detail showing several ears of wheat often carved in low relief, high relief or inlaid. This motif can be seen on Hepplewhite and Sheraton pieces.

Wheel-back A Baltimore side chair made 1820 to 1840. The design derived from an ancient Roman folding chair. The distinctive feature is the circular "elbow" at the junction of the stiles, side rails, and rear legs.

White wood Natural or unfinished wood.

Whitewood American poplar wood, used for structural purposes and japanned and painted piece.

Whiting Crushed chalk used to raise japanned decorations in the American William and Mary period.

Whorl foot A foot carved in the shape of an upcurved scroll. Seen on various Chippendale pieces. These also appear on Victorian pieces with a French rococo flavor.

William and Mary period American William and Mary Period 1690-1720 (English William and Mary Period 1688-1702)

Key Words: wood patterns, open carving, walnut, marquetry, cup turnings, "S" and "C" scrolls, caning

The Dutch influenced William and Mary style was dramatic and vital. It had highs and lows, thicks and thins, positive and negative designs, colorful designs, and more slender forms than the Puritan style. It was a great change from the preceding Puritan period that was architectural solid oak furniture. with flat incised carving.

American William and Mary furniture was less bulky, less formal, less decorated, and smaller than its English counterpart. It was not less exciting.

This furniture is not as sturdy or durable as the Puritan furniture. The pieces I see are often wobbly and the veneers are often damaged.

One piece that did not conform was the kas. This was an enormous Dutch style wardrobe with heavy doors and large bun feet. They were often paneled and had applied molding. Some were painted with fruit, ribbons, birds and flowers. While not consistent with the period they were dramatic and colorful too.

This was the period that introduced veneer to American furniture. Veneer is a thin layer of wood glued to a base wood. Veneers do not hold up like solid wood. William and Mary furniture was made primarily of walnut and maple, but of course local woods were also used. This is the first American period to appreciate wood grains. Red gum that was also called bilsted was used for many early painted chests and kases. Few pieces have survived because gum was a soft wood.

Decorative burls and fancy grain veneers command attention in this period. Veneering was the major decoration on William and Mary walnut furniture.

The herringbone pattern was very popular and the walnut markings, growth forks, stumps and burls yielded beautiful veneers for William and Mary furniture.

Plume designs of oyster veneers, which are concentric circles, of walnut, yew, elm, and mulberry, are English.

By the close of the 17th century inlay and marquetry arrived in the colonies, via Holland, France and England. Marquetry had been introduced into England from France. Contrasting inlays were referred to as marquetry. Marquetry is actually a sophisticated form of veneering. On English pieces there is endive or seaweed marquetry which has delicate arabesque flowing lines. Marquetry with ivory, dyed woods, or bone are likely to be Italian or Continental, but not English or American.

The William and Mary period saw the beginning of lacquering (japanning) of maple pieces in the Oriental style. Americans actually saw few examples but immediately admired this colorful decoration. The lacquer work of this period in America and England is coarse and thin. Japanese lacquer was thick and was highly polished. Japanese artists used forty to fifty layers of lacquer sap while the English used one or two. Americans used less. The favorite American palette was a blue-green background with red and green designs and gentle gilding. Greenish-blacks and browns as well as tortoise were also used as background colors. On rare occasions lacquered designs are seen on bare wood. The chinoiserie designs came from Oriental porcelains or design books. English pieces were primarily in vibrant vermillion and glowing green, but also in yellow and blue. The English also made black pieces. They added varnish to their ground colors for brilliant brown and tortoise-shell backgrounds. English pieces used gesso to raise the chinoiserie designs. American pieces do not have varnish added to their ground colors and did not pad their decorations with gesso. Occasionally whiting (crushed chalk) was used under the designs. English pieces have heavy decoration and heavy gilding. American pieces are simpler. English japanned pieces may be seen on heavily carved and gilded gold and silver stands, occasionally with a matching carved and gilded pediment placed on top of the piece. In America, Boston was noted for fine japanned pieces.

The shallow incised carving found on Puritan pieces was replaced with dramatic deep-pierced carving. Examples are seen on cane chairs and bannister-back chair crest rails. William and Mary furniture is immediately recognized by bold trumpet and inverted cup turned legs resting on ball or bun feet. English inverted cup turnings sometimes were decorated with pierced carving similar to the Oriental ivories the English so admired. American cup turnings are solid and plain. Trumpet turnings in America are rarer than cup turnings. Inverted shallow cup turnings (of little depth) are usually English.

Various pieces have cabriole legs which are new to this period and are so important in the Queen Anne period which followed.

This style was exciting to people accustomed to square architectural furniture. Especially the open carving and bold

Flemish scrolls in stylized "C" and "S" scrolls on legs, chair crests and stretchers.

Other legs were ball, ring, vase, spiral, or block turned with curved, shaped, crossed, or flat crossed stretchers. The spiral or twist turnings are associated with Philadelphia and New York furniture. Legs on highboys are about 20 inches from the ground and are spirally turned or trumpet turned and braced with flat or curved stretchers.

The carved Flemish scroll foot known as the Spanish foot or Portuguese paintbrush foot is found on chairs and tables (example: tea tables). The Spanish foot also appeared on the new easy chairs. A Spanish foot without a backward curve is called a brush foot. Spanish feet on cabriole legs often had a carved or applied "ankle" bracelet. The Spanish foot was design-influenced by Oriental bound feet.

Important pieces in this period were the flat topped highboys, lowboys, daybeds, slant-topped desks, gate-leg tables, secretaries, corner chairs (roundabouts) and the easy chairs.

William and Mary highboys are flat-topped and finished with molded cornices. In the Queen Anne period they will be larger and may have a broken pediment. In England the word "tallboy" is used in place of "highboy". (I wonder why they didn't call their lowboys "short boys"?) The word "highboy" is said to be of American origin. English tallboys sometimes had double-domed tops. American highboys did not.

The highboy is a chest of drawers, evolved by placing a five or six drawer oak chest on a frame table, that could be reached without stooping down. The stands or lower portion are usually of the same wood as the upper portion. The stands usually have six trumpet turned, spiral turned, or "C" scroll legs about 20 inches from the floor, connected by flat, shaped, crossed, flat crossed or curved stretchers. Shaped rear stretchers are rarer than straight ones. Late highboys may have only four legs. Few have survived due to this weaker construction. An ornament called a "drop" may indicate the previous placement of the two legs no longer used. Late highboys may have the new cabriole legs. The stands have one long drawer or two or three smaller ones. Some stands were painted or stained dark. The upper portion has at least four drawers. The highboys were often veneered only on the front to cut the cost. The bases are around 37 inches long. New teardrop brasses are usually seen on these pieces.

The lowboy served as a dressing table or as a table for flower arrangements. Many more lowboys have survived than highboys. Late lowboys and highboys may have the "new" cabriole leg, often with the Spanish foot. Some wear applied "bracelets" at the ankle of these legs. Highboys are greatly valued because they are rare as well as beautiful.

English tallboys and lowboys are usually larger and taller with elaborate marquetry; some have rosewood and syca-more inlays. American examples are plainer. Some English tallboys had extremely thick and heavy twisted legs. Our lacquered highboys are much simpler with less chinoiserie and thin gilding.

The oval gate-leg table was the most popular table and is frequently mentioned in inventories of this period. Some have walnut tops and fruitwood legs. Some have Spanish feet. Most have vase turned legs or occasionally ball and ring turned legs. Drop-leaf tables were also made. Butterfly tables were made in the late 17th century. The term "butterfly" refers to the shape of the supporting brackets. The edge of these tables was usually slightly rounded. The drawer, if there was one, is wider at the bottom. These tables had raked turned legs attached to trestles or raked turned legs with turned stretchers. Butterfly tables are rare and valuable and uniquely American. Some William and Mary tables are found in maple wood instead of walnut. Some are painted entirely in black or red. The tea table appears in this period but becomes more important in the Queen Anne period. Rare tea tables are seen with stone tops.

English gate-leg tables of this period were frequently inlaid with fruitwood and often had spiral twisted legs. Baluster turnings above cabriole legs are English. Splay legged "cricket tables" or tavern tables, some with a platform can be

American or English. English William and Mary table tops made from a Chinese lacquered panel can be seen.

In the William and Mary period the chest of drawers was established as a piece of furniture. These early chests of drawers often had applied molding in geometric designs that were mitered at the corners. Applied molding appears earlier on Puritan chests. The chests usually have four drawers and there is always a pronounced projecting base mold. These chests have ball or bun feet. There is often a reel turning above the ball and often a collar at its base. The new cast teardrop brasses appear on some of these chests. Drawers with lips came in about 1700. Painted chests of drawers without applied molding and not jappaned are seen with designs similar to needlework in New England.

William and Mary chairs begin to acquire curved backs, an Oriental influence which replaced the stiff straight Puritan chair backs. Certain chairs referred to as "cane chairs" (canning is another Oriental gift) had elaborate Flemish "C" and "S" scrolled crest rails, legs and stretchers with pierced carving. These chairs also had pierced carved crest rails (top rails) with cane backs and seats. This type was the American version of the English cane chair which was a version of the Flemish cane chair. Some were painted black. English cane chairs were often made of beechwood. In America, beech was rarely used but some American cane chairs were made of fruitwood or maple. English cane chairs often have carved animal feet, but American ones do not. Late English cane chairs often had square cabriole legs. American cane chairs did not. Late cane chairs may have a scalloped skirt. Flemish cane chairs were more elaborately carved than English. English cane chairs were more elaborately carved than American. As cane seats replaced earlier less comfortable rush seats, leather replaced the cane ones. On leather seats and backs, brass tacks were used to secure the leather. The leather was laid vertically.

A less expensive leather chair called the Boston chair had a simple arched crest rail and Spanish or paint brush feet. Squabs, which are loose cushions, were used on all seats in this period.

Caned and scrolled daybeds, some with hinged backs, are new in this period. For persons used to simple seating, this must have been the ultimate in luxury. Daybeds were called "long chairs" or couches.

The banister back was another important William and Mary chair. This chair was less expensive than the cane chair and very popular. The banister back usually had a rush or splint seat, block and baluster turned front legs, block shaped rear legs, baluster turned front stretchers, and three to six slats or turned or split banisters which were mortised into the bottom or stay-rail and the crest rail to form the back. Sometimes the slats were reeded. The crest rail was often beautifully decorated. Some crest rails have pierced carving, using heart and crown decoration or double-arch or yoke-back motifs. On the back posts, may be seen finials in acorn, knob or double knob turnings. The legs may sport Spanish feet, doubled feet (a double round turning), turnip feet, knob feet or just the sausage turned leg. The banister chair was made as an armchair as well as a side chair. Sometimes the arm-roll was pierced. About the year 1700, saddle-back reeded banister chairs are seen. These had a concave top rail.

The corner chair (roundabout) puts in its appearance at this time and will become more popular in the Queen Anne period. Winged slat-backs are seen around 1670. Many with an important crest rail.

Corner chairs with scrolled slat-backs appear about 1710. Slat-back chairs continued to be made.

A new piece is the easy chair. This was an upholstered chair, usually with a curved back or arched crest back, block and vase turned front legs terminating in Spanish feet with plain block shaped back legs, and with a removable seat cushion. This type of chair had a turned stretcher. The upholstered wings kept the draft or fire heat off the user. This chair was upholstered in fabrics like serge and shallow. It was a great luxury. This is probably the first truly comfortable chair made in America. The use of slipcovers comes with upholstered furniture.

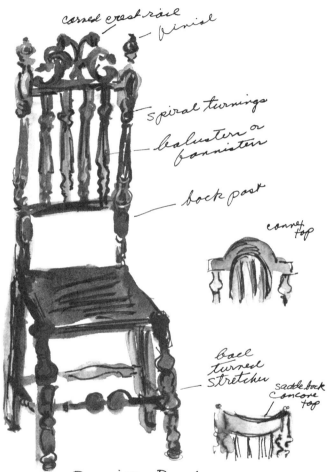

carved crest rail
finial

spiral turnings

baluster or
bannister

back post

convex
top

ball
turned
stretcher

saddle back
concave
top

Bannister Back
William and Mary 1700
Boston Massachusetts
maple - painted black

cushion or squab used
on chairs

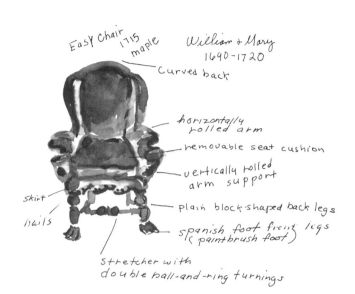

Easy Chair 1715 maple

William & Mary
1690-1720

Curved back

horizontally rolled arm

removable seat cushion

vertically rolled arm support

plain block-shaped back legs

spanish foot front legs
(paintbrush foot)

skirt

nails

stretcher with
double ball-and-ring turnings

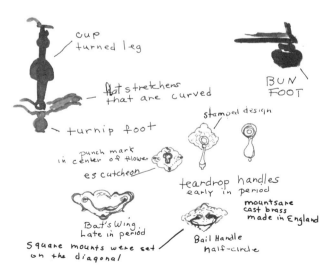

cup
turned leg

BUN FOOT

flat stretchers
that are curved

turnip foot

stamped design

punch mark
in center of flower

escutcheon

teardrop handles
early in period

mounts are
cast brass
made in England

Bat's Wing.
Late in period

Square mounts were set
on the diagonal

Bail Handle
half-circle

The slope or slant-top desk appears also in this period. First as an upward lifting sloped box on a frame. Then as a slant or slope top desk on a turned table frame with one or two drawers, open on the bottom, and frequently with crossed stretchers with a finial where they crossed, and subsequently as a top to a chest of drawers. Slant-top desks often had secret compartments for hiding gold coins. These slant-top desks have large bun, round turned, and turnip feet. In England, the chest type slant-top desk was called a bureau.

Slant-front secretaries with solid upper doors also appear in this period. The English secretaries often used mirrored glass on their doors. American secretaries had bracket feet, bun feet or short cabriole legs with Dutch feet. The English secretaries often had looking glass in their pediments as well as on their doors. American secretaries were plainer but not "plain". The English secretaries often had double domes. American William and Mary secretaries are very rare.

(Mounts) The handles on William and Mary furniture were wooden knobs or cast brass teardrop brasses. The brasses often had designs chased, punched or stamped on them. Brasses are an Oriental influence. The brass teardrop handle is the earliest brass handle and was made about 1690. These early handles were attached by wires (cotter pins) clinched on the inside. The wire strips of iron were called tangs. Posts came a little later with handmade nuts, always of irregular shape. These brasses were a light yellow color. The brasses were removable and kept bright by polishing. Remember how dark it is in houses after sundown. Any reflecting surface caught the light from the fire or candles and was enjoyed. At this time, most light came from fire, candles or lanterns, as ceiling light was rare, and brasses reflected their light and provided a counterpoint. The Museum at Winterthur thus exhibits American furniture of this period only with simulated candlelight.

Most brasses in this period came from England because colonial brass foundries were forbidden by the English parliament. English producers of cabinet brasses cultivated the American trade before and after the Revolution and issued elaborate catalogues. It was actually a lucrative "mail-order" business. Of course the colonies produced some metal work.

In addition to the brass handles, there were good sized brass keyhole escutcheons, made of a similar design but with more elaborate chasing, or stamping or punching. At the corners or near the rim are four holes for the brads which are brass nails by which they were attached.

Another brass handle which came later in the period was the bail handle. This handle is a half oval pull attached to a stamped plate by cotter pints at both sides. I have seen early English pieces with round mounts and bail handles. This handle had large, matching key-hole escutcheons, also attached with brass, like the teardrop escutcheon. After 1720 teardrop handles were out of style and bail handles were in. These remained popular until 1825.

(Important William and Mary cabinetmakers) Some known makers of William and Mary pieces were Thomas Dennis, Nicholas Dibrowe, John Allis, Samuel Belding and John Hawkes.

(Woods) The William and Mary period is called the age of walnut. Walnut and maple were the woods used most often. The walnut seen in early American furniture is characterized by a light brown or grayish brown color, similar to English and French walnut. It will gray from exposure to sunlight. American walnut is more difficult to work than is the European. This timber has a handsome grain and may show markings of stripes, waves, and mottled figures. Irregular growths, crooks, forks, stumps and burls yielded prize veneers for William and Mary furniture. American walnut, though harder to work, is considered finer than European walnut because it can withstand the damaging furniture beetle.

Virginia walnut was exported to England, and English furniture in this period was often made from it. Therefore, a William and Mary piece made of Virginia walnut can be English.

Maple was also used; primarily rock or sugar maple, which grew throughout the eastern half of America. Maple can be a light creamy tan to a deeper pinkish tan. It is a hard, strong wood, and has a fine texture. Maple has very interesting grain figures described as fiddle-back, curly, tiger-stripe, and bird's eye.

Red gum was also called bilsted. It is moderately strong and straight grained but dents easily because it is a soft wood. Red gum takes a good polish. It was used for early William and Mary painted chests and for kases. Few pieces have survived.

Rosewood came from Brazil and Madagascar. The colors range from yellowish-tan to orange and deeper and red tones to a very dark purplish color. It has brownish-black or black pigment figures and can display ivory streaks. It was used for inlay on English pieces.

Sycamore is a hard wood with dense grain like maple. It is sometimes quarter-sawed to accentuate the flecks in the grain and used as a veneer for banding. It takes a high polish and when finished is a very light brown. Stained greenish-yellow, it was known as hare-wood by English cabinetmakers.

Willow brasses   Brass mounts with plates that are baroque scrolled in outline. They were also made in open pierced patterns. Many late Queen Anne and Chippendale pieces, including block-and-shell pieces have willow brasses. Block-and-shell brasses are unusually large.

Windsor chair   Also called Philadelphia chairs. These first appeared in the Queen Anne period. They included the low-backs, with backs formed by flattened arms that curve out at the ends with an applied arm at the rear (the low-backed Windsors were the forerunner of the 19th century captain's chair). The comb-back has a back resembling a comb, formed by a combination of the spindles through the arms terminating in a comb piece. The fan back has spindles that fan outward to the crest-rail or comb piece. The fan back was also made with a braced back. The continuous arm Windsor has the back and arm formed by one piece of bent wood. The writing arm Windsor has a pork chop shaped piece attached to the right arm. These were often made with a drawer beneath the writing surface. The rod back Windsor has spindles that may not curve backwards and may be bamboo turned with simple crest-rails. A variation is the coop-back which has a geometric cage design between the flat top rail and the second rail. The arrow back has a back made with flattened spindles resembling arrows. Various early Windsors had upholstered seats secured with tacks.

Windsor rocker A regular comb back with rockers, said to have been invented by Benjamin Franklin. A uniquely American design!

Wing chair An upholstered chair from about 1700 in America with a high back and side wings. It shielded the sitter from drafts and fire heat. With upholstered chairs came slip covers. Americans used them to protect their upholstered pieces. Also called a fireside chair.

Winged claw A heavy Empire foot often found on sofas. Shaped like a winged animal claw with carving at the knee.

Winged monopodia supports Winged animals, dolphins, griffins, or giant wings seen on Empire pieces as legs. Examples on Empire sofas and tables.

Winged orbs A decorative Egyptian motif of winged disks or eyes. Examples found on American Victorian Egyptian style pieces.

Winged paw An animal foot with winged carving appearing on its knee. These were seen in the Empire period.

Work table A table made in the last half of the 18th century for womens' sewing tools. Examples are Hepplewhite and Sheraton pieces often of mahogany in Philadelphia and tiger maple in Ohio.

Writing arm A wide wooden piece, curved on one side, attached to the right arm of a chair for writing. Examples seen on various Windsor chairs.

"X" form stretcher A stretcher which joins the legs in a way that forms an "X". These are seen in the William and Mary period. Also called a satire.

Yoke back Another name for a Queen Anne hoop-back chair.

York chair   A Queen Anne chair with a straight conical version of the cabriole leg ending in a pad foot. Examples made in New York.

MORE AUCTION TIPS

Do not pass up auctions which don't specialize in the furniture you collect. You may find just what you are searching for, at a reasonable price, hidden among the featured furniture. For example, you may find an isolated Federal piece available at an auction billed as featuring "country", for a price much less than would be the case if other Federal collectors were bidding against you.

Call an auction house after a sale to see if unsold pieces are available below the original reserve. You would still be responsible for the auction house commission. Individual auction house policies would dictate any possible procedure. The owner of any piece in question would have to be consulted and agree.

COLLECTING AND BUYING

Antique American furniture is an extension of our national and personal character and reflects the proud heritage of a democracy. The collector of antique American furniture is in essence "a keeper of the flame".

Visit Winterthur in Delaware, the Metropolitan Museum in New York, the D.A.R. Museum in Washington, D.C., the Smithsonian Museum in Washington, D.C., the American Museum in Britain, near Bath, the Museum of Fine Arts, Boston, Massachusetts, the Museum of the City of New York, the Art Institute of Chicago, Illinois, or cities like Charleston or Philadelphia. Not only will you see fine furniture in authentic settings but acquire a thirst for American history and have a wonderful time too.

While it is a privilege to own antique American furniture, it can also be expensive. The fortunate have inherited this special furniture or acquired it when the prices were lower. But some of this fine furniture does not cost hundreds of thousands of dollars. *You can find good pieces if you are willing to search out shops and attend auctions. The very best has hit the million dollar mark but there are still treasures for you at the same prices as new furniture.* The more expensive the furniture, however, the more cautious you must be in your selections. The temptation to forge is strongest for expensive pieces. It does not pay to fake the less costly variety.

Year sold (The following are all auction prices unless otherwise indicated.)

1876	Victorian Renaissance revival walnut	
	bedroom suite plain bedstead	$7.00-13.00
	Elegant nine footers	150.00
	Unfinished beds start at	5.50
	Marble top bureaus with mirrors were	23.75-59.50
	Bureaus without toilets (mirrors) were	8.00-10.00
1876	Walnut veneered sideboard circa 1860,	
	marble	36.00-90.00

1991	Walnut veneered sideboard circa 1860	5,900.00
1960's	Rococo revival sofa mid 19th century	100.00-200.00
1981	Similar piece	600.00
1990	Similar piece	2,000.00
1990	Similar piece (These pieces are lower than what you would pay for an ordinary new sofa)	1,600.00
1960's	Chippendale cherry block-front chest, less than	10,000.00
1991	Similar one Similar one (but different quality)	165,000.00 47,500.00
1962	Sheraton bow-front chest circa 1820	4,500.00
1991	Similar ones from	5,000-25,000.00
1962	Federal card table circa 1820	292.00
1990	Similar table	4,500.00
1962	Chippendale wing chair circa 1780	900.00
1976	Similar chair	3,200.00
1991	Similar chairs	6,000-7,000.00
1962	Chippendale serpentine sofa circa 1780	1,650.00

1991	Similar sofas start at	3,500.00
1960's	John Jelliff open-arm walnut sofa circa 1860	200.00-300.00
1991	Similiar sofa	1,870.00
1981	Chippendale slant-front maple desk circa 1780	1,900.00
1990	Similar desk	6,600.00
1981	Victorian walnut secretary	1,250.00
1991	Similar piece	1,950.00
1981	Empire circa 1815 classical carved mahogany card table	800.00
1991	Similar piece	2,000.00

When you find what you love and can afford the piece, BUY IT! Later may be too late and *timing is everything.*

The Puritan period is handled by only a few select dealers or at an auction. There was little to start with and less now.

William and Mary pieces are more available but often require extensive restoration. Highboys, chairs, tables, and chests still turn up and you might acquire them for less than the later Queen Anne or Chippendale pieces.

Although examples of Queen Anne and Chippendale furniture are the cream of American craftsmanship, the ebb and flow of life sends them to market like all other furniture. Don't believe you can never afford a Queen Anne or Chippendale piece. The secretaries and highboys may be out of reach but many other pieces may not. Some prices at the close of this chapter will illustrate what I mean.

Export porcelain, oriental carpets, and "of the period" glass and ceramics are important accents. Fresh flowers are nature's gift to everyone.

The Federal periods, Hepplewhite, and Sheraton, might be a starting place for the new collector. Hepplewhite is rather formal. Except for dining room pieces, it is not widely coveted at the moment. With classical architecture starting to regain interest, this furniture will soon be in greater demand. Sheraton furniture is perhaps the most available as I write. It is handmade, sturdy, colorful, and charming. You may not get Duncan Phyfe, but this antique furniture can be less costly than new repro's or just new furniture.

Empire furniture is America's furniture stepchild, but is recently gaining appreciation. Its lines are simple. White marble tops and deep storage spaces are beginning to appeal to the discriminating buyer. The scrolled center tables are modern in character. The "very French" black cabinets with plaques and ormolu are getting a new audience that find them beautiful. They are certainly a focal point for any room. With a good eye for proportion, you can successfully incorporate Empire pieces into many furniture schemes.

The later Victorian pieces are now even more in demand. Furniture from between 1840 and 1910 offer the collector *everything*. This is the period of revivals. Puritan (colonial) or Jacobean revival, Elizabethan, Renaissance, and Greek revival to name a few. As with every period various pieces are always expensive. A Belter piece will sell for more than a simple rococo one. Right now aesthetic furniture and Stickley pieces are going up in price. When Barbra Streisand shops Stickley, people listen, and when Oprah Winfrey buys Shaker, it too ascends. I would predict that Shaker holds its value while the arts and crafts pieces probably will not.

Each year furniture auction prices reach new highs. The other side of the coin is that many fine pieces do not even sell. These pieces may have "your name on them". We collectors must make a concerted effort to find what we desire. An "Andy Warhol shopper" is singular. Most collectors spend a lifetime poring over catalogues, just looking, and slowly acquiring one piece at a time. Make an effort to know dealers and appraisers on a personal level.

The 1990's are going to be a pairing-down time. True values will be more important than just acquiring more and more. I am always surprised at how little early Americans had in the way of furniture. Now even our bars have couches. I believe the 1990's will be the beginning of people sitting up straight again and perhaps the demise of the "couch potato".

Fine new furniture is very expensive. Various museum reproductions cost more than actual antique furniture. I love old pieces and I want them to look old.

I have listed below various past and current auction prices of American antique furniture. There are still possibilities for you.

These figures show how the value of antique furniture has appreciated over the past decades. Keep in mind that good antiques can be found at prices no higher than quality new pieces. Compare some of the numbers listed above with contemporary museum reproductions, such as a Newport secretary which sells for $24,000, or a Federal desk going for $6,000. As I've shown, a good reproduction of a Philadelphia wing chair in 1991 is available at $4,000. Surely a genuine antique piece is nicer to live with than a museum reproduction. Another plus is that you don't have to worry about nicks and scratches. They're already there.

1982	Sheraton mahogany two part secretary	$4,125.00
1991	Similar piece (surprisingly) (Is now the time to look for Sheraton?)	4,000.00
1982	A pair of Chippendale, mahogany side chairs	4,600.00
1991	One Chippendale mahogany side chair Another piece	24,200.00 3,250.00

(Wide range here)

1982	Cherry circa 1740 candlestand	500.00
1990	Similar piece	6,000.00
1990	Similar piece	900.00
1990	A refinished cherry Shaker candlestand (Somebody got a great bargain. They are out there.)	2,600.00
1991	Egyptian revival pedestal Egyptian revival chairs can cost more than 18th century chairs	600.00
1962	New England mahogany card table circa 1820	295.00
1991	Similar piece	1,000.00-2,000.00
1964	A Queen Anne drop-leaf table circa 1730-40	1,250.00
1991	Similar piece	4,500.00
1964	An American mahogany sideboard circa 1820	875.00
1991	Similar pieces	4,000.00-6,000.00
1976	A Queen Anne maple highway sold circa 1750	6,000.00

1990	A Queen Anne mahogany highboy circa 1740	7,000.00
	What does a mahogany Baker piece sell for?	
1977	Windsor brace-back chair	325.00
1990	Similar piece	1,100.00
1977	Federal mahogany breakfast table	850.00
1991	Similar table	2,700.00
1977	Empire carved mahogany sofa	160.00
1990	Similar piece	8,000.00
1981	William & Mary Highboy, 18th century	1,990.00
1990	Similar piece	2,300.00
1981	Federal mahogany sideboard	4,600.00
1991	Similar piece	16,500.00
1981	Hepplewhite chest, French splayed feet	1,600.00
1990	Similar piece	2,600.00

SELLING

While acquiring antiques we love is a pleasure, disposing of them can be a problem. The treasure now becomes a mere object. *Do not ignore the challenging adventure of selling.* The value of stock investments may be determined on the day they are sold. Antiques give pleasurable dividends while you live with them and give a good return on investment when intelligently sold.

You have choices when you decide to part with your possessions. *Do not settle for an inadequate price from a local shop just to get the piece or pieces out of the house.* Someone in your family probably worked to get the best price when the price was acquired. Don't be content with less than the best price when you sell. Too many people give away their antiques. Don't be in a hurry.

What is the "market value" of your antique? You can't sell effectively if you do not know its worth. Look in shops carrying similar antiques. Go to antique shows. Call in an appraiser. I have gone to homes to appraise one piece and said "What about that one"? The reply was, "that old thing"? That particular old thing was an Arts and Crafts lamp with a singular shade worth a small lottery prize. At the very least look at a current price guide. Consider your options carefully. *Do not be lazy.* Selling wisely puts money in *your pocket* where it belongs.

One choice is to offer it back to the original place of purchase. Most antique dealers are delighted to recover an old piece they have already once profitably sold. You might make a deal for cash, or the dealer might take it on a consignment basis, or take your piece in trade for a different piece. I hope you have saved the original invoice. Any transaction should be in writing.

Consignment means allowing a dealer to sell on your behalf for a percentage of the sale price. You own the object until it is sold. If you put the piece *on consignment, get the terms in writing.* Remember, the piece is yours until sold. Deal only with a person you trust to inform you of the price actually received. Only leave your piece at a shop that has a fast turn over. Otherwise, it could sit until you are nearly as old as the antique. The terms agreed upon should be on the shop's letterhead and dated and signed.

Donations can be a fast route if you need a tax write-off. Check with your accountant. In 1991 the government is allowing museum donations at "market value". Some charities will provide you with a receipt indicating value that will be acceptable to the Internal Revenue Service. Everything is worth something to someone.

Auctions are another option. Do you have an auction house nearby? Call them. They will put you in touch with an expert dealing with your type of antique. They will even send an expert out to your home if necessary. Ask questions. Talk about reserves.

If you are not near an auction house, write to one or more, describe your piece and enclose a clear photograph and a copy of your original bill of sale if you still have it. You will hear from them. Most auction houses are very good about getting back to you.

If you believe you have a rare piece or collection consider contacting the big auction houses in New York. If you agree to a sale, consider putting a *reserve* price on the item or collection. If a catalogue is printed, you may wish to have a photograph included at your cost. *What a thrill to see your treasure hammer down a grand price.*

Classified ads are an alternative choice. Are you willing to allow strangers into your home? A small piece might be shown at your bank where they have special private rooms, or in your garage. *Do not be alone in your house with strangers.* I have met lovely people and bought through their ads but I have never run an ad for myself.

Whatever arrangements you make, consider the physical welfare of the piece or collection. Wherever or however you dispose of your antiques by sale, or gift, be sure they remain in good condition and in good hands. Everything in life is lent to us and we in turn should see they will be available to future generations. That is the moral responsibility of the antique collector.

FINAL WORDS

If I have any advice it is "never have a home without a dry basement or snug attic" because whatever you buy, your mother bought, or your grandmother bought, or your great grandmother had, it will come back into style and be valuable to someone.

BIBLIOGRAPHY

American Antique Furniture, E. Miller - Barrows and Co., New York, Vol. 1 & 2

American Antiques, Cynthia & Julian Rockmore

American Country Furniture 1780-1875, Ralph and Terry Koval - Crown Publishing Co., New York

American Furniture, Doreen Beck - Hamlyn Publishing Co., New York, London, Toronto, England

American Furniture, Helem Comstock - Viking Press, New York

American Furniture, Jonathan Fairbanks & Elizabeth Bates - Richard Marek Publishing Co., New York

American Furniture, Charles Montgomery - Viking Press, New York

American Furniture and the British Tradition to 1830, John Kirk - Alfred Knopf, New York

American Furniture from the Kaufman Collection - J. Michael Flanigan - National Gallery of Art, Washington Distributed by Harry N. Abrams, Inc., New York

American Furniture in the Metropolitan Museum of Art - Morrison H. Heckscher, published by the Metropolitan Museum of Art and Random House, New York

American Furniture 1680-1880 From the Collection of the Baltimore Museum of Art by William Vos Elder III and Jayne Stokes

American Heritage, Robert Athearn - Dell Publishing Co., New York, Vol. 1

The American Heritage Dictionary - Dell Publishing Co., New York, New York

The American Heritage History of Antiques from the Civil War to World War I - American Heritage Publishing Co., Inc.

American Painted Furniture 1660-1880, Dean Fales, Jr. - Dutton and Company, New York

Antique Collector's Guide & Reference Handbook

Antique Fakes, Raymond Yates - Gramercy's Publishing Co., New York

Antique Furniture, L. A. Ramsey, Helen Comstock - Hawthorn Books, New York

Antique Monthly, June 1990, John Jelliff by Mildred Jailer

Antique World Magazine, May 1980

Antiques Magazine at 1973 - George Heakels

Antiques World Magazine, May, 1980 - Gathering of Fairbankses Design from Boston, Virginia Bohlin, Milo Naeve

British Furniture, Margaret McDonald Taylor - G. P. Putnamiss Sons, New York

The Collectors Glossary of Antiques and Fine Art, John Bernasconti - Walker & Co.

Colonial Homes, September, October 1982

The Complete Encylopedia of Antiques, L. A. Ramsey - Hawthorn Books, New York

Directory of Historic Cabinet Woods, I. Hinckley - Crown Publishing, New York

Discovering Antiques, Volumes 19 & 20 - Greystone Press, New York, Toronto and London, edited by George Harper - George Harper Publisher, New York

Early American Furniture, John Kirk - Alfred Knopf, New York

Early American Rooms, John Sweeney, A Winterthur Book - W.W. Norton & Co., New York

Early Victorian Connoisseur Period Guides, Ralph Edwards and L. Ramsey - Reynal & Co., New York

The Easy Expert in Collecting & Restoring American Antiques - Mareton Marsh - J. B. Lippincott Co., Philadelphia & New York

Encylopedia of Antiques - Mandarian Ltd., Hong Kong

The Encylopedia of Furniture, Joseph Aranson - Crown Publishers, New York

English & American Furniture, Herbert Coscinsky & George Hunter - Garden City Publishing Co., New York

The English Chair - M. Harris & Sons, 44 New Oxford Street, London

English Furniture, John Rogers - Spring Books

English Furniture of the 18th Century, Herbert Coscinsky - The Waverly Book Co., London

English Furniture Styles 1500-1830, Ralph Fastnedge - A. S. Barnes & Co., New York

Field Guide to Early American Furniture, Thomas Ormsbee - Little, Brown & Co., Boston

Furniture - Century Furniture Co., Grand Rapids, Michigan

The Furniture Doctor by George Grotz - Doubleday and Company, Inc. - Garden City, New York

Furniture in Maryland 1740-1940 - The Collection of the Maryland
Historical Society by Gregory R. Weidman

Furniture Masterpieces of Duncan Phyfe, Charles Cornelius -
Doubleday, Page & Co., New York

Furniture Treasury, Wallace Nutting - MacMillian Co., New York

The Gentle Art of Faking Furniture, Herbert Cescinsky - Dover
Publication, New York

Genuine Antique Furniture, Major Arthur de Bles - Garden City
Publishing Co., Garden City, New York

A Guide to American Furniture, Van Lennep

Handmade in England, Sigmund Lavine - Dodd Mead & Co., New
York

How To Know American Furniture, Robert Bishop - E.P. Dutton, New
York

Identifying American Furniture, Milo Naeve - The American
Association for State & Local History, Nashville, Tennessee

Images of American Living, Alan Gowans - Lippincot Co., New York &
Philadelphia

International Book of Wood, Mortyn Bromwell - Simon & Schuster,
New York

Know Your Woods, Albert Constantine, Jr. - Home Craftsman
Publishing, New York

Lecture at Art Institute by Donald Fenmore, Assistant Curator of
Winterthur on American Metals, February 7, 1988

London Arts & Antiques, June 1982

The Magazine Antiques - May 1985 Authenticating American
Eighteenth-Century furniture, by Harold Sack

Make Your Own Antiques by Francis Hagerty - Little Brown and
Company, Boston - Toronto.

Marketplace Guide to Victorian Furniture, Peter Blundell & Phil
Dunning - Collector Books, Paducah, Kentucky

Masterpieces of Furniture, Verna Cook, Sclomonsky - Dover
Publications, Inc., New York

More American Furniture Treasures, Lester Morgan - Architectural
Book Publishing Co., New York

New England Furniture as Williamsburg, Barry Greenlaro - Colonial
Williamsburg Foundation, University Press of Virginia

19th Century Philadelphia Cabinet Maker by Kenneth Amber

An Outline of Period Furniture, Katherine McClinton - Clarkson Palter Inc.

Pictorial Price Guide to American Antiques, Dorothy Hammond - E.P. Dutton, New York

A Place For Everything - The Henry Francis du Pont Winterthur Museum - Winterthur, Delaware

Random House College Dictionary

Shaker Furniture, Edward D. Andrews & Faith Andrews - Dover Publications, New York

Smart Money and Art - Martin S. Ackerman

The Story of American Furniture, Thomas Ormsbee - MacMillian Co., New York

Three Centuries of American Furniture, Oscar Fitzgerald - Prentice Hall, Inc. - Englewood Cliffs, New Jersey

Treasury of American Design, Clarence Hornung - Abrams, Inc., New York

Victorian Furniture, Robert & Harriett Swedberg - Wallace Homestead, 1912 Grand Ave., Des Moines, Iowa 50305

Victorian The Cinderella of Antiques, Carl Drepperd - Doubleday & Co., Garden City, New York

The Windsor Style in America - Charles Santore Running Press, Philadelphia, Pennsylvania

Woods We Live With, Nancy & Herbert Schiffer - Schiffer Limited, Exton, Pennsylvania

The World Book Encylopedia - Field Enterprises

World Furniture, Noel Riley, Octopus Books Limited, London

INDEX